THE PASSWORD IS COURAGE

Charles Coward was one of the most extraordinary sergeant majors in the annals of the British army. Leader of his *Stalag*, he was a modest hero and a determined survivor who ingeniously planned and carried out many escapes from prison camps. But his greatest successes came inside the barbed wire barricades.

At Auschwitz he daringly planned an underground army . . .

THE BANTAM WAR BOOK SERIES

This is a series of books about a world on fire.

These carefully chosen volumes cover the full dramatic sweep of World War II. Many are eyewitness accounts by the men who fought in this global conflict in which the future of the civilized world hung in balance. Fighter pilots, tank commanders and infantry commanders, among others, recount exploits of individual courage in the midst of the large-scale terrors of war. They present portraits of brave men and true stories of gallantry and cowardice in action, moving sagas of survival and tragedies of untimely death. Some of the stories are told from the enemy viewpoint to give the reader an immediate sense of the incredible life and death struggle of both sides of the battle.

Through these books we begin to discover what it was like to be there, a participant in an epic war for freedom.

Each of the books in the Bantam War Book series contains a dramatic color painting and illustrations specially commissioned for each title to give the reader a deeper understanding of the roles played by the men and machines of World War II.

THE PASSWORD IS COURAGE

JOHN CASTLE

BANTAM BOOKS · TORONTO · NEW YORK · LONDON

*This low-priced Bantam Book
has been completely reset in a type face
designed for easy reading, and was printed
from new plates. It contains the complete
text of the original hard-cover edition.*
NOT ONE WORD HAS BEEN OMITTED.

*A Bantam Book / published by arrangement with
Souvenir Press Ltd.*

PRINTING HISTORY
*First published in the United States in 1955 by
W. W. Norton & Company, Inc.
Bantam edition / September 1979*

*Maps by Alan McKnight.
Drawings by Tom Beecham.*

All rights reserved.
Copyright © 1954 by John Castle.
*This book may not be reproduced in whole or in part, by
mimeograph or any other means, without permission.
For information address: Souvenir Press Ltd.,
43 Great Russell Street, London WC1B 3PA, ENGLAND*

ISBN 0–553–12132–4

Published simultaneously in the United States and Canada

CONTENTS

"The fact that a British prisoner of war had to show the German defendants what moral courage involved is a matter of regret to the Chamber as a German Court."

From the Court Judgment,
Wollheim v. I. G. Farbenindustrie,
Frankfurt (Main), 1953

1

CAPTURED

Again, he looked at his watch, holding it close to his eyes until the hands were just discernible in the faint light from the window. Outside, a damp gray mist swirled slowly off the marshes, huddling the little white houses of Stadt-Bau closer together and masking the rusted barbed wire of the compound behind it. There was a movement as a sentry stamped the rawness from his feet; a cough; then silence.

The man at the window listened intently. No sound came from the room above him: evidently the *Wehrmacht* were sleeping well after their evening wine. The watch hands crept to one o'clock exactly. He waited a moment longer; then knocked lightly on the floor, once.

In a black, evil-smelling washroom below him, fifteen British soldiers nudged each other and tensed for action. Two of them felt their way on to the rough wooden sink and heaved at the concrete slab roof. With a sudden creak it yielded as the joints in the brickwork, previously chipped loose, broke away. Quickly it was levered back and wooden staves fitted to prop it open. One by one, without a word, the fifteen men hoisted themselves up, scrambled out, and dropped to the grass outside.

It was the work of a minute, but to the man above it seemed an age. He watched the men until the mist swallowed them, and imagined them pressed to the ground before the sentry returned on his beat.

They should now be at the place where the perimeter wire had been loosened. Forcing himself to be quite still, he counted the seconds, sharing with the men outside the almost unbearable strain of inactivity. This was the crucial point, the knife edge of freedom or disaster, when success and perhaps even lives hung on the accuracy of his timetable, the result of weeks of lonely observation and plotting of the guards' movements. This was the moment when everyone in the band of helpers —the document forgers, the compass makers, the map draughtsmen, the tailors, the men who fashioned incredible tools from old tins, those who had kept watch and those who had contributed rations—waited in the dark anonymity of their bunks and steeled themselves for the blasting crack of rifle shots, the shouts, the clump of boots and crashing of doors that meant failure.

At the window of his room, with an instant release of tension, he had counted the guard passing twice, and still no sound. They had made it. Fifteen away, now separating into their pre-arranged singles and pairs; if the wire had been replaced as carefully as he had instructed them, discovery of the break with all its uproar might not come till morning. He climbed back into bed, chilled through but happy. "Good luck, blokes," he whispered. "Keep your heads down." If any of them managed the unlikely journey to England they would be sure to visit a house in Lower Edmonton, London, and say with a grin, "Hello, Mr. Coward. Charlie sends his love, and says to tell you he'll be over soon."

Those now partly shattered London streets had been Charles Coward's home. For him, as for most Cockneys, manhood had come quickly, and to a sturdy, healthy youngster, enlistment in the Army appealed as a splendid way in which to spread one's wings; by 1924 he had completed a tour of service in India and returned to take up the threads of civilian life. Before long he had thrown up his job to start business on his own, managing a small shop, but a speedy accumulation of bad debts defeated the venture. In his spare time he found release and expression in organizing dances and concerts for a number of charities: the stage and the chance it gave to project himself, proved an irresistible attraction. Because he so obviously enjoyed himself, he pleased his audiences.

Nevertheless, the Army was not forgotten, and when in the fateful summer of 1939 it became urgent overnight to muster every available soldier, he was among the first to be called into full service. Back in his old regiment, the Royal Artillery, he instructed for some months at a camp in Hereford, chafing under the boring conditions and being, one suspects, a good deal more easygoing with the trainees than instructors are generally supposed to be. Some of the friendships he formed then last to the present day, for when the time came for him to say goodbye to his lads he asked to be posted with them to France. Somewhat to his surprise, the request was granted. Surprise, because of the Services' uncanny ability to send a man to where he would rather not go, and to ignore his own personal preferences, especially in wartime. However, Coward was lucky. He would say that he has always been lucky.

So it was that when Hitler launched his big attack in the spring of 1940, Coward was with the men he had helped to train, the sergeant major of a battery fighting a desperate rearguard action and suffering heavy casualties

They had reached the outskirts of Calais one morning when a burst of small arms fire sent Coward and some of his men diving into a café from where they could use their rifles. Several hours passed, during which he received a wound in the leg and another in the head while doubling across the road to report to his officer. Then, taking advantage of a lull, he attempted to review the position. It was far from comfortable. The Germans were between them and the port of Calais, and to try to fight their way through such a concentration was clearly an impossibility. Wearily he pondered on the next move to make; but the decision was taken out of his hands. Bouncing into the café came a hand grenade, and within two seconds it was all over. For the Germans who followed, those of the Britishers who were still alive, stunned and momentarily helpless, were an easy capture.

Coward's prisoner of war career had begun: a career that was to make him a principal troublemaker for the Hun and to transform him from an ordinary ebullient Cockney into an extraordinary amateur espionage agent. A thousand men taken prisoner would learn gradually to accept the inevitable; they would attempt an escape, fail, and then decide quite logically that the scales were weighted too heavily against them. Coward could never do that. From now on the war was for him a personal affair and a challenge to his wits.

Even as the German soldiers burst into the café, waving their guns in the faces of the dazed survivors, his one thought was to escape.

All the prisoners from that section of the town were assembled into a long line, yet another column to begin the trek to Germany. At first a march was an almost enjoyable relief, but after two or three hours came fatigue; at the end of eight hours the exhaustion was crushing. The men were given neither food nor water. If any dropped out of line they risked being summarily despatched with a bullet. The Germans, flushed with victory, had no time to waste on wounded prisoners at that stage of the war. They marched until the order came at last to halt. Then everyone slept until morning light, when it was time to form up again.

When two days had passed without food, Coward began to get a little light-headed. The head wound seemed to affect his spine, which ached and gritted with every step, and the gash in his leg painfully obstructed movement. He realized that much more would finish him. He had to get away. And he did, that same night.

The column had stopped for sleep, the men slumping down anywhere in collapse, their bodies covering the grass verge of the road and lining the sides of a ditch. Cautiously, Coward looked around at the guards. They had obviously relaxed, hardly expecting any of their utterly spent charges to be capable of escape, and were talking and laughing together in a group. He ripped off the conspicuous bandage from his head, rolled down into the mud of the ditch, and began to wriggle slowly away from the crowds of prostrate men. He passed within feet of the chattering Germans, not daring to emerge until he was well out of sight and earshot. Crawling with difficulty, stopping frequently to regain his strength, he made his way across a stubble field to where the silhouette of a farmhouse cut into the night sky. A hasty reconnaissance revealed the friendly shape of a haystack; with a final effort he clambered up its side, burrowed himself into its softness, and fell asleep.

He remembered no more until warm sunshine awoke him. Scarcely knowing where he was or what had happened, he lay for a little while listening to the unaccustomed sound of hens clucking and the measured clop-clop of a horse's hooves on gravel. They held no meaning for him. Beneath his eyelids the world receded to a pin point, a white speck dancing to the rumble of distant engines. Converging shafts of light stabbed at the speck, always missing it but somehow impinging on a voice speaking faintly and unintelligibly from the uttermost reaches of consciousness. With a start, like an animal that has smelt danger, he raised himself on an elbow and opened his eyes, screwing them up against the brightness of the morning. Stiffly he swung his legs over and slithered down the side of the stack, landing with a jar that sent him sprawling on the ground.

His mind did not question the fact that hands other than his own were helping him to his feet. Before him stood an elderly woman, her eyes wide with shock. As best he could, he conveyed to her what he was, and in a few minutes was once more sitting on the hay, this time consuming with the hunger of a wolf a hunk of bread and bottle of coarse red wine brought him from the farmhouse. Immediately he felt better. He regarded almost with benevolence the friendly scene about him and was slow to realize that the kindly Frenchwoman, beside herself in agitation, was motioning him back to the top of the stack.

He made it just as the accelerating roar of motorcycles sent the hens scurrying for safety, and in another moment the yard echoed to the bedlam of engines and guttural commands. There was nothing he could do, he told himself, but to wait and to rest. The brief meal was already having its effect and very soon he was sleeping soundly.

So soundly that an excruciatingly loud noise almost in his ear did not rouse him for a moment. But when it did, he recoiled in alarm. A large dog had jumped up beside him and was snarling and barking practically in his face. In vain he made some attempt to quiet the brute. The barking increased, German voices called to the dog from below him, then a bayonet began to prod up into the hay.

When the soldier with the bayonet saw what he had flushed out, he was speechless for a moment. Not so Coward, however, who expressed in a few terse and succinct phrases of Anglo-Saxon origin his extreme distaste of the whole proceeding.

His annoyance increased when the excited soldiers surrounded him, bellowing with laughter. It came to him then what an extraordinary apparition he was: tattered, literally covered with mud and grime, hair matted with blood and bits of hay. The humor of it appealed to him and he joined in the merriment until a light tap from a rifle restored the *status quo*. Then he sobered up and paid some attention to the questions addressed him by the *Unteroffizier*. A curious exchange followed, with neither side having better than the sketchiest notion of what the other was saying, but at length Coward gathered that he was being asked if there was anything he would like. Nothing at that moment seemed more desirable than a wash and as soon as the Germans had grasped this there were nods and grins.

With a flourish the *Unteroffizier* led the way to a large cattle trough and gestured Coward to refresh himself. The dirty water was something less than appealing, but at least it would remove some of his grime and perhaps he could bathe his wounds. He was about to plunge in his hands when a chuckle from one of the soldiers made him straighten up suspiciously.

"What's coming off here?" he demanded.

A sharp blow caught him in the back, someone gripped him around the waist, and with a great splash he was in the trough. It was bitterly cold. To the accompaniment of shouts of laughter, he tried to find a firm handhold on the wet surface only to be thrust under again, kicking and spluttering and gasping for breath. The entertainment appeared likely to continue indefinitely; then Coward was aware that all was quiet and he could pull himself upright. Fixing him with a humorless stare as he sat in the water was a German officer. Coward's glower was by now humorless too.

"Go on, split your bloody sides," he told him.

If the officer understood, he did not answer. Giving a curt order, he had Coward hauled as unceremoniously out of the tank as he had been dumped in. The treatment was not calculated to dispel Coward's truculence and it was only with the greatest difficulty that he restrained himself from registering his feelings in a more violent way. It was not long before he was put astride the pillion of a motorcycle and driven by a grinning German at breakneck speed to the nearest marshalling point of prisoners of war.

The spectacle he presented there, soaked through and shivering, was for the dejected Tommies a sight for sore eyes. Yet again there were hoots of laughter.

"Christ, it must be bath day!"

"Did a U-boat get you, sir?"

"Good thing his missus can't see her hero now!"

If Mrs. Coward could have seen her husband in his present state, perhaps even her concern for him would not have prevented a smile. Who could foretell that this bedraggled specimen, standing miserably rebuffing the merriment of his comrades while water dripped on his boots, was a born escaper and an incredibly astute patriot, a man to be known in the course of time as the Count of Auschwitz and who, not content with tormenting the Germans for five long years, was to return even after the war and face them as an important witness in their own criminal trials?

2

WINNING THE IRON CROSS

Soon after rejoining the column of marching prisoners, Coward began to suffer horribly. Perhaps the splinter of steel embedded in the muscle of his thigh had injured a nerve for the pain in his spine had become acute and before long a paralysis started to spread over the lower half of his body. In desperation he managed to drag himself along, well knowing the consequences of dropping out of line. The column struggled on, ever slower, yet somehow covering mile after weary mile. Jokes were fewer now, each man intent on keeping up with the plodding boots in front of him, but those nearest Coward helped him as best they could. But the morning arrived when he found it impossible to stand by himself, and he knew then that the end had come.

Still he would not give in. They had spent the night in a huge barn just inside the German border, and when the men were ordered outside to prepare for another day's march he rolled aside to a corner in which hay had been stacked and contrived to cover himself with a bale. The guards neglected to give more than a cursory glance around the barn's malodorous interior; they were almost as tired as the prisoners, though presumably not so hungry, and in a few minutes they had set the column on its way and its sound was growing gradually more distant.

Coward moved himself and tried to sleep. It was a forlorn hope. The pain of his wounds and the worry that he should do something to make his position more secure, made sleep unthinkable. To remain where he was would be highly dangerous, yet the slightest effort increased his misery. He sank into a sleepless torpor filled with fantasies of home.

He awoke to sounds of activity, the whine of a truck bumping in low gear over the rutted field outside. It was dusk and he peered into the shadows, trying to make out the uniforms of several men who presently entered the barn bearing stretchers. A dozen or more casualties were laid on the ground, two or three of them carefully lighting cigarettes and talking quietly in German. The more seriously wounded were lowered gently on to the hay and lay there groaning or in silence. The air began to reek of iodoform and dried blood.

In spite of his discomfort, Coward felt a rather bitter appreciation of his position. He knew he must be urgently in need of medical attention, but the last few days had shown that little compassion could be expected from the enemy. Yet the German army had always enjoyed a reputation for fair treatment in the First World War. Was their present indiscriminate butchery of all who stood in their way merely the lusting of a madly advancing army not yet under proper control, or had Hitler bred a new type of fighter impervious to any international rules or decencies? Coward chose to believe the former theory.

Laboriously, once darkness was complete, he edged himself over to the nearest man, who appeared to be unconscious, and lay beside him. A number of blankets had been distributed around, and one of these he pulled over himself. His guess was right; eventually, by the dim light of lanterns, food was brought in. Eagerly he received his ration, gulping down the coarse bread and sausage as gratefully as if it were the choicest fish and chips from his favorite shop at home. Indeed, it may well have been, for his fevered imagination was once again in London, and the night passed in fitful dreams.

With the daylight came the medical orderlies. They lifted the wounded back on to the stretchers and Coward found himself being carried out into bright sunshine and pushed aboard a large open truck. There were five of these, and the drive in convoy was as rough and alarming as any given Coward by a seaside roller coaster in peacetime. For several hours they lurched along, sliding the stretchers from side to side, and with his face to the sky he could gain no idea of their direction.

It must have been afternoon before the trucks swung into a forecourt and stopped. A chatter of voices followed and Coward had his first experience of the much-vaunted German efficiency that seemed to entail endless discussion before even the simplest operation was performed. Then gentler hands lifted him out and German male nurses bore him quickly into what was evidently a civilian hospital of considerable size. As they traversed the startlingly clean and disinfected corridors it was increasingly clear that it was in use as a base hospital for the fighting fronts. Only servicemen were to be seen, one or two of them giving him a casual glance as he passed by.

His two bearers reached a large ward, stepping carefully over the polished floor, and deposited him on a bed. Removing his boots, but not attempting to take off his clothes, they threw a blanket over the one he still clutched, and left.

"What now?" thought Coward.

On either side of him and opposite were beds, some of whose occupants seemed not long for this world, several of them with limbs suspended in various forms of traction. Within a few minutes his immediate neighbor began to address him, asking a question. Coward stared back, hoping he gave the impression of shellshock. It apparently succeeded, for the man put a cigarette in his hand and offered him a light. Coward drew the smoke into his lungs with relief and grinned in thanks at the German, wondering anxiously if his khaki-clad arm had been noticed as it emerged to take the cigarette. No, all was well; his benefactor was calling out to other patients and pointing to Coward's head. They looked at him commiseratingly, those who could move at all, then returned to the contemplation of their own misfortunes.

After an hour or so a white-coated orderly came up and stood beside the bed. He produced a printed form and pencil. Coward held his breath.

"Der Name bitte?"

This was clear even to one who did not speak the chosen tongue, but Coward decided not to push his luck too far. He let the orderly ask again, and then muttered:

"Karl . . . Karl Joseph."

"Karl Joseph," repeated the orderly. *"Und Nummer?"*

Completely floored Coward gaped at him, growling inarticulately and rolling his eyes. The orderly stood for a moment in utter astonishment. Then a solution appeared to dawn on him. Shaking his head, he made an entry on the form and turned away.

Left to himself, and sweating profusely, Coward knew that discovery must certainly come soon. The first demand for his identity book, or wash, or examination by a doctor, must reveal him. Yet none of these things occurred. The whole ward seemed preoccupied with something else; there was a mounting excitement as bedclothes were straightened, lockers tidied.

The swing doors to the ward burst open and in marched a resplendent procession, headed by two smartly clad German N.C.O.s whose brightly polished field boots clacked sharply on the parquet flooring. At their heels strode two tall officers, one sporting a straw-colored Hitler mustache, the other pale-faced with a scar stretching from beneath his right eye to his chin. Behind them, escorted by two more officers, smaller than the first pair but more heavily braided, strutted a curiously small plump general of the *Wehrmacht*, red tabs matching his scarlet features and a long trenchcoat of oiled silk reaching almost to his boots like a nightshirt.

There was a shout of *"Achtung!"* from a *Feldwebel* and the patients sitting up immediately stiffened in salute; those who were flat on their backs, Coward among them, went rigid in their beds like so many corpses. Striking an impressive attitude the officer with the scar then delivered a short but vigorous speech, referring to the general in obvious compliment from time to time, and with frequent emphatic allusions to the Fatherland and the Führer. Everyone paid the closest attention and Coward watched in fascination, the macaber aspect of his own position almost forgotten. Several male nurses had now crept into the ward and were listening in awe.

With a resounding *"Heil Hitler!"* the speech came to an end and the general, with his henchmen following, began to waddle around the beds. After a few words and handshake with each patient, he would pin a glistening medal on the counterpane. Coward realized dully that he was about to be awarded the Iron Cross.

The cortège slowly approached, leaving in its wake a row of proudly smiling soldiers. Then Coward looked up to find the general looming over him and extending a pudgy hand.

"So, geben Sie mir die Hand."

Limply, Coward responded, feeling the German almost fondle the khaki cloth around his wrist. The General turned to one of his officers, murmuring sympathetically, and when he faced Coward again the familiar decoration dangled from the striped ribbon in his hand.

"Das Eiserne Kreuz—so!"

Coward nodded and watched unbelievingly as the fat fingers fastened the medal in front of him. In a moment the general had moved on to the next bed.

When everyone in the ward had been served there was a final heel-clicking and the distinguished warrior and his courtiers left, presumably to where further scores of heroes awaited his felicitations. A babel of voices broke out at once as the soldiers hastened to unpin their crosses and congratulate themselves upon their acquisitions. Coward, in his relief, felt an impulse to roar with laughter and smothered his face in the pillow. This would be something to tell the boys, a story good for a pint for many a long year.

His merriment was short-lived. An orderly shouted *"Achtung, der Arzt!"* and a doctor entered, making with a determined air straight for his bed. This was it. He braced himself for the inevitable exposure.

The doctor was speaking to him, but receiving in reply only unintelligible sounds that seemed to take the form of English cuss words. The doctor paused, considered, then rapped out an order to the man at his side. It was clearly to strip Coward for examination. The orderly stepped forward, pulled back the blankets, then stopped, wavering in uncertainty. The doctor stared incredulously, the man in the next bed stared with popping eyes, everyone stared in silence at the lone figure lying there in bed in all the full panoply, albeit dirty, of a sergeant major of the British Army.

In the pandemonium that followed, it would have been impossible for Coward to have answered any questions even if he had understood them. Almost dancing, beside himself with rage, the doctor screamed and spluttered, rounding on the cringing orderlies as if to strike them. The ward seemed full of people talking and shouting at once. More nurses and other officers came running in, adding their meed to the confusion of reprimand and denial. To Coward it seemed that the entire hospital had gathered around him and were gesticulating in his face. Only the general and his aides were absent, for it was obviously in the interest of nobody's health to break the news to them.

When the first frenzies of the pantomime were over, he pointed to his back and said *"Kaput,"* the sum total of his German. Instantly this unleashed a renewed performance from the doctor, the crowd drawing back a few paces in alarm. Leaning forward as far as he could, Coward grinned at him and held out his hand.

"Be a pal, chum. Give me a fag."

The doctor's neck swelled; then, barely controlling himself, he swept out of the ward. With a visible effort another officer took command, ordering the spec-

tators away. Coward fell back on his pillow in resignation to await the tramp of boots that would surely an-
nounce his removal under guard.

It came, some fifteen minutes later—minutes
spent assuming a nonchalance he did not feel—but to
his great surprise, the soldiers who entered and approached him in amazement, carrying between them a
stretcher, were British.

"Stap me, it's a sergeant major."

"Where did you get that Iron Cross, sir?"

"Never mind that," said Coward. "Get me out of
this loony bin before they cut my throat."

"Easy on then. We'll soon have you over the
road."

The three beat a triumphant retreat, ignoring the
outraged looks directed at them, and a short walk
brought the puffing bearers to a small prisoner of war
camp adjacent to the hospital. It was made up of
prisoners of several nationalities, nearly all of them
wounded and undergoing treatment before being sent
to regular camps. Nearby was the town of Coblenz on
the Rhine.

The rigors of camp, even one devoted to wounded,
were a far cry from the comforts of hospital. In two
long barrack-rooms with three-tier bunks, a couple of
British Army medical officers did their best to tend the
injured with inadequate supplies and instruments, but
Coward was overjoyed to be back with his countrymen. When he had washed and been comfortably settled in under three gray blankets, his wounds were
inspected and declared not serious. He felt for the moment at peace with the world and dozed off with English voices in his ears and quiet in his heart.

Under care the paralysis began to leave his back
and legs. The wounds were healing satisfactorily, and
as health returned his thoughts turned once again to
the tantalizing prospect of escape. He waited impa-
tiently until he was quite fit, his only indisposition being the hunger pains that always accompany the first
few months of captivity. Then one day, without pre-

meditation, he simply took down from its peg a doctor's raincoat, put it on, walked out of the gates without challenge.

It was a foolish attempt, of course. He was not equipped to escape. For hours he wandered aimlessly through Coblenz, always stopping short of the check barriers at the bridges across the Rhine. There he watched the police at work and it occurred to him that once having inspected a driver's pass they never looked inside his vehicle. Here surely was a ray of hope. He walked hurriedly up and down the streets looking for a suitable truck, finally selecting a ramshackle contraption with a canvas cover. A glance around him and he was clambering inside, crawling over an unsavory load of filthy sacking and empty boxes.

Shortly after nightfall someone climbed into the front cabin and with a violent shaking and series of backfires the truck got under way. Hardly had it done so before the rising wail of sirens heralded an air raid. Coward cursed miserably and fluently. He felt no elation when the truck stopped only momentarily at a check barrier, knowing that the driver would pull up at the first convenient shelter. This was only a matter of yards, and uncomfortably close to the bridges which were prime targets, but his chances seemed better in the truck than to run for it, so he curled himself on to the sacking and prepared to spend a cold and wretched night rocked by bomb blasts.

Dawn was streaking the sky when the covers were thrown back and an astonished driver discovered his thoroughly chilled passenger at last dropping off to sleep. Too cold to say or do anything, Coward watched him fumbling for an ancient brass whistle, its piercing shrieks reaching, it would seem, to Berlin itself.

His appearance before the camp *Hauptmann* was short and inauspicious.

"You are stupid," declared that worthy. "For why do you escape with officer coat, eh?"

"I wasn't escaping," said Coward indignantly. "I was taking a stroll around Coblenz last night when the air raid alarm sounded. I didn't know where the nearest bunker was and the lorry was handy so I hopped in. I couldn't break the law by not taking shelter, could I?"

The *Hauptmann* looked at him hard and long.

"Very well," he rasped. "But not to leave the camp again. Go!"

Coward thanked him cordially and went.

The long train steamed slowly through Germany, wending its leisurely way past towns and villages, through fields of ripening crops where peasants straightened their backs for a moment to wipe the sweat from their chins. Across roads and past gates it went on, stopping sometimes in a siding while some faster passenger train passed, but always working its way east to where the broad plains of the agricultural region of the *Reich* stretched out to join the sweeping steppes of Poland.

Filling the ancient wagons were British soldiers. Thirty or so were crowded into each truck, sprawled about the dirty floor and talking, singing or just lost in thoughts of home. From one grille, high up in the side of its wagon, a mouth organ ground out the strains of "Nellie Dean," the ballad competing with the steady rumble of the wheels.

For days the snaking line of trucks had borne their miserable freight, days in which boredom and hunger possessed the men as they scratched together little heaps of straw on which to ease their cramped limbs. At the rear of the train was a comparatively luxurious wagon reserved for the use of the German guards; it could boast windows and a stove, and within it the worthy Teutons played cards or read, waiting with typically bovine patience for the journey to end. Behind this wagon, at the very end, trundled one that housed, in a high glass box overlooking the length of the train, the railway guard. Equipped with whistle, brass horn and gorgeous uniform, his eminence sat there in lonely splendor like a prize exhibit at Tussaud's.* However, at this particular time he was in somewhat somnolent mood, his lunch of sausage and brown bread making him drowsy and longing to succumb to a good nap. The retreating line of track had a restful, hypnotic effect, the symmetry of gleaming rails and evenly spaced sleepers being marred only by an occasional sliver of wood. The guard found himself watching for these pieces to appear and then following them lazily with his eyes as they passed slowly out of sight. In spite of himself, he was intrigued. Who could be wasting good firewood like this, and so much of it too? There was another piece just sliding away under the train and now a whole stretch of scattered fragments of wood. *Ach,* it was probably one of those accursed French wagons falling to bits up in front there. Be lucky if there were anything of them left at all by the time they got to . . .

Then he snapped awake. He grabbed for the air-brake and jammed it on, feeling with relief the driver respond. The train ground to a clanking halt, heads appearing at the windows of the guards' truck.

A red-faced *Feldwebel,* followed by a score or more soldiers, hastily joined him. They stumbled along the cinders, peering under each wagon. Eventually, they found what they were looking for.

Great jagged lumps of wood hanging between the wheels of one wagon. The *Feldwebel* swung himself up, pulled over a heavy iron bar securing the door, and slid it open. What he saw made his eyes bulge and brought a flow of strong invective to his lips.

Thirty or so men sat innocently against the walls while in the center of the floor gaped a large hole through which they had clearly intended to disappear at the first convenient moment. They all seemed surprised and concerned when the *Feldwebel* pointed out to them this structural defect. They inspected it gravely.

---

*Famous London wax museum where lifelike historical figures are dramatically displayed.

"It's not safe."

"Last time I travel on this perishing railway."

"Must be bleedin' mice," said a little Cockney who was still sucking at a splinter in his finger.

They leaned back and watched the fireworks as the German literally danced. His antics called to mind the spirited performances of the dervish, and were commented upon by the Englishmen with admiration.

"Should be on the 'Ackney Empire,"* remarked the Cockney, who had perhaps said enough for the time being.

As the German began to calm down he turned to a figure reclining languidly in a corner, his head pillowed on grimy straw.

"You—you are in charge, *ja?*"

"Yes," said Coward, "I'm the British Camp leader—or was."

"Who did this? Who wrecked the wagon? Sabotage!"

Coward shrugged. "It's a German-built wagon. They're coming to pieces all the time. Don't blame us."

Giving it up, the *Feldwebel* ordered them out and distributed them among the other already overcrowded trucks. As the engine began its long haul once more, the mouth organ resumed its recital. This time the tune was a popular hymn, but with an undercurrent of unusual noise. A little later darkness fell on the lonely track, and with it, at intervals, sundry sticks of wood. The whole train was hard at work.

They had left Limburg one dreary morning after a particularly early roll call at which the Britishers had been separated from the other nationalities and herded in squads to the railway station.

Coward was not sorry to go. Limburg was a stinking place, only fit for animals and the constantly gnawing hunger was preying on his spirits. The end of his stay there had been especially unpleasant, relieved only by one serious scrape with the Germans, and at the end by

---

*An English vaudeville theater.

being brought from solitary confinement in the "cooler" to testify at the court-martial of a German who had beaten him up for his part in an escape pulled off by a group of Polish prisoners. In Coward's rucksack now were several medals handed him at a clandestine ceremony by members of the Polish community in memory of that episode.

When the rather unruly mob had boarded the train at Limburg, the guards had somehow omitted to make fast one of the truck doors on the far side. To escape was impossible, but it was the work of a moment to toss a handful of lighted straw into the wagon of an adjacent train. Within a few minutes there was a splendid blaze and as they steamed out they had the inexpressible joy of seeing flames and sparks reaching up to the station roof. It was a royal send-off, gladdening their hearts for the wearisome ordeal that lay ahead.

Hungry men cannot conserve food as others can, and the ration of one loaf and chunk of *Wurst* apiece had soon gone. No more food was forthcoming. The unsecured door had been discovered at the first of the periodic checks, and before long the occupants of that wagon were wishing they had attempted escape back at Limburg Station, even though the chances of success were infinitesimal. By the sixth day many prisoners were weak and ill, praying for an end to their chicken-coop existence. Sometimes the train would be stationary for hours, at others it would progress only at a crawl.

On the evening of the seventh day the doors were rolled back and the men roused to their feet. Outside lay the platform of a dark and gloomy station, dimmed lights shining on the bayonets of waiting guards. The men crowded forward, speculating wildly on where they were. Then someone caught sight of a signboard in the shadows and to his mates spelt out the word that would remain with them to the end of their lives: "Lamsdorf."

3

THE CANADIANS

Once again the shuffle through the darkness to a vast camp, the hurried searching by experts, the empty palliasse, the thin spoon and rusty dixie. Coward's heart sank; everything seemed to be the same as Limburg. Was this to be another great international pool like the other? The mob of men were guided through the darkness to a large compound and divided up to various huts. They threw themselves on the hard bunks and slept, tired out and sick at heart.

Lamsdorf, however, was a British camp and soon to grow into the largest *Stalag* in Germany. Built in 1915 as a camp for British prisoners captured on the Western Front, it had been called into service again in World War II and once more echoed to the sound of English dialects. Later on, around 1943, it was to house some 12,000 prisoners, some of them a floating population of workers, and it formed the base for the operations of men such as Coward.

He quickly adapted himself to the way of life in the camp and was soon the confidant and helper of the two British Camp Leaders, Warrant Officers Sherriff and Lowe. These two men had in their quiet way built up an organization to vigorously represent the rights of the men, provide an almost unbroken news service direct from the B.B.C., and assist hundreds to make their escape attempts, some of them actually reaching home after many vicissitudes.

The *Stalag* was on a vast plain, flat as a deal board, bounded on one side by a seemingly limitless coniferous forest, covered with deep snow in winter and alive with swirling dust storms in summer. A huge bite had been taken out of that forest as it joined the plain and filled with a great mass of barrack huts. This was Lamsdorf, *Stalag VIIIB*, the home for six years of Britishers from all parts of the Commonwealth, where Palestinians lodged in friendship with Arabs, Canadians rubbed shoulders with Australians, and Sikhs shared their meagre space with Gurkhas. English, Scots, Irish, Welsh, New Zealanders, South Africans all mixed in one mighty hotchpotch, their outside feuds and misunderstandings lost in the boredom and comradeship of the immediate present.

Six compounds, each of six barracks, made up this gigantic cauldron of monotony and fortitude, together with an annex designed for the German administration offices and the post office. A large arid field inside the camp served as a sports ground and one of the barracks had been converted into a makeshift theater and school. In each barrack lived between 150 and 160 men in three-tiered bunks. These blocks of bunks occupied most of the space in the dismal buildings, which were long and so low that the men on the top tier could barely sit upright in bed without brushing their heads on the ceiling. Two tiled ovens of ancient vintage reared their bulk in each barracks and served as a place to lean on, for rarely was there enough fuel to light them. Half a dozen tables and forms completed the picture and comprised the entire home for the men.

Here they lived and slept and ate. Here they read, shuffled the cards, talked, argued, planned escapes, yawned away their existence. Here were spent years of many lives.

Many of the men at Lamsdorf were skilled in some kind of work and wherever possible they would try to follow their avocation, creating for themselves little worlds of reassurance. Lucky was he who had been a school teacher in Civvy Street, for he could forget himself in taking classes. Fortunate too were the men who liked to carve; if they could bribe a guard to bring in a knife they were set up for months. The card players would gather in their cliques and find mental escape in the intricacies of bridge. Always, however, remained the hard core of prisoners who could pass their time in doing none of these things, but clung to thoughts of home and loved ones, ruminating on the might-have-been until only by the greatest effort of will could they preserve a show of spirit to their fellows. For them there was only the question "How long, how long?" and very often the preparations for a mad escapade that too frequently led to death.

To this unhappy melee Coward brought the innate chirpiness that was to carry him through many hard times. He chummed up with the little Cockney who had commented on the activity of mice in the train, and the pair of them managed to make life at least bearable for themselves. They helped with the radio set that lay hidden in the straw of a certain corporal's palliasse, policing the environs of the barrack every night at nine while operators of the crazy contraption tuned in to London. Made up of an assortment of wires and several old tubes illegally scrounged by men on working parties, it was concealed in a cardboard box and spent its nights under the corporal's toes. From its wheezy depths could be heard the golden chimes of Big Ben and the familiar voice of the announcer as he read the evening news. The main points were hastily scribbled down and then repeated in each barrack of the compound. The faces of the listening men were often grim; Dunkirk was only a memory but the night bombing offensive on Britain was bitter gall, making each man strain at his confinement. Coward managed to keep extraordinarily buoyant. He would emphasize at least one item of encouraging news each night, and when this was not forthcoming from the B.B.C., would fabricate it himself with cheerful unscrupulousness.

Yes, in those early days Lamsdorf was a dark, dreary place, a pit of despair and hunger for its thousands of inmates. But soon a livelier note was to be struck, one that would infuse new life into the men and put back the sparkle into their eyes. It came with the spring of 1941, a spring gloriously welcome after the freezing cold of the winter, and on a Monday morning bright with thin sunshine and renewed hope.

"Seen the carts?"

The Scouse's cry from the doorway rang down the barracks. The card school stopped. Heads turned.

"What flippin' carts?"

"The carts—loads of 'em coming in."

"If they're taking us away in carts now," said a dour Scotsman, "I'm applying for my discharge."

"Shut up!" shouted The Scouse. "They're piled up with cases—come and see."

"Cases?" said Coward. "Perhaps they're parcels from home. Come on!"

Cards abandoned, the men scampered out, leaving the Scotsman ruefully examining his hand. "First blasted run I've had at Lamsdorf," he groaned.

Outside, men were running from all directions to gape at a number of rickety carts drawn by weary horses and driven by even wearier and more emaciated Russians. As the caravan wound its plodding way, excited rumors swept through the camp, reaching a fever pitch when over the loudspeakers came the order to muster parade. Within two or three hours every man was gleefully unpacking the very first Red Cross parcels, to be shared a quarter each. This became the weekly ration, then supplies gradually improved until a full parcel every week was the recognized issue, bringing peace and contentment. Coward pooled his with The Scouse, a common practice making for economy and greater variety. The first cup of tea brewed from the two-ounce packet in the parcel was a holy rite, the stirring of condensed milk a scientific operation; real tea, such as they had drunk all their lives, seemed to bring England into the gloomy hut and infuse their existence with grace.

The parcels brought simple luxury beyond belief; only later did the idea occur that they could be put to other uses that would transform camp life.

Off and on, Coward spent some few years in this camp, returning to it between seasonal jobs in charge of working parties. But always on his return there were new stories awaiting him, like that of Shorty and Jock. Shorty was a huge, gangling, good-natured Londoner who had for his inseparable companion a diminutive Scot; something in their two personalities had fused together, and strangely enough in a place where tempers were frayed at the least provocation, they had never been known to exchange a hard word.

One day in the summer of 1942 the two were walking along the main road that dissected the camp, and drawing curious looks from the men within earshot, for they were arguing hotly. The cause of the quarrel was never known, but Shorty was seen to suddenly lash out and strike Jock, who tumbled into a ditch alongside the road. As he lay there, quite unconscious with blood streaming from his mouth, Shorty was overcome with remorse. He leaped down to his pal and tenderly lifted his head which rolled helpless to one side. Shorty looked up at the faces around him.

"I've killed him," he said quietly. "I've killed Jock."

No one spoke, though most of those present knew that Jock was only knocked out and would live to see many another day dawn over the Silesian landscape.

Shorty got slowly to his feet and walked away. They watched him go, still incredulous that he could seriously think he had killed Jock. The tall, pathetic figure shambled along the road, straight for the high wires surrounding the camp's outer perimeter. Arriving at the wire, he began unhurriedly to climb, tearing his hands on the barbs and ripping his uniform at every move.

Amazed, the guard perched up in the nearest postern box roared at him to stop.

Unheeding, Shorty struggled higher.

The guard's indecision was frightful. He bellowed again, staring as if hardly able to believe his eyes while Shorty straddled the top of the wire, let himself painfully down on the far side, and picked his way across the intervening coils to the outer wire. Then he reached up, found a handhold, and put his weight on the strands again. As they sagged he slipped, but hanging on tightly he had practically reached the top once more, moving with deliberate slowness, when the air split with the thunder of machine-gun fire. His body jerked and shivered under the impact, slithered down two or three feet, then hung in mid-air on the barbs. It remained there for two days until the camp leader obtained permission to have it lifted off. As surely as anyone, Shorty had died for his ideals.

None of the people who witnessed the tragedy will ever forget it, but suicides were not uncommon at Lamsdorf. Shorty, grotesque on his harsh Calvary, had acted on impulse. There were some who premeditated cunningly to die; occasionally one strove to crucify himself in a burst of exhibitionism. Such a case was a certain Paddy whose attempts, for reasons he would never disclose, were ludicrous in the extreme. One of his methods was to stand beneath a postern box and hurl obscenities at the guard above, always to fail because his Irish was incomprehensible to the German. Another was to try to hang himself from the goalposts during an international soccer match, only to be cut down hilariously by a crowd from the three thousand spectators. Eating messes of saccharine tablets would often fatally affect the heart, but in Paddy the only result was violent vomiting. At last, however, he achieved his aim. The Germans had recently installed water reservoirs for use during air raids, and after being missing for some days, Paddy was found embedded in the ice in one of these.

Burials were conducted with reverence and solemnity, and were well respected by the Germans who share with many an East End housewife the love of a

"good funeral." The coffins were interred with full military honors in the cemetery at Lamsdorf village, about a mile away, the carriage being swathed in a huge Union Jack. Now this was the only chance for the British to show themselves off to the German populace and, with due acknowledgment to the seriousness of the occasion, they took full advantage of it. As many men attended as were allowed, scrubbed and polished, with a brass band and a full company of Scots pipers playing lustily on instruments received from the Red Cross in Geneva. Marching to the cemetery, they delivered the Dead March in *Saul* and other suitable laments, but on their return they were allowed to play any music of their own choice, with the exception of the British National Anthem. This was their opportunity and the villagers were regaled with the stirring strains of "Rule Britannia," "Land of Hope and Glory," "The Bluebells of Scotland" and a selection of other patriotic pieces. It became quite a show for the civilians and they would turn out in force to view the mad Britishers marching smartly past, brass gleaming and the kilts of the Jocks swirling. The German delights in a good military show and the boys gave them just that. The impressive turnout of the men made such a contrast to the drab, dirty, patched uniforms of the Germans that it must have been noticed by the people; at any event, it was known that the camp *Kommandant* had bitterly harangued the guards on their slovenly appearance and advised them to copy the demeanor of the British.

On the daily camp parades, the men would go to the extreme, affecting indifference to their captors, by lining up in every assortment of dress and undress. Early one morning, clad in this way, all the Canadians taken in the Dieppe raid of 1943 and the entire complement of the R.A.F. were mustered in their compounds to face what appeared to be the whole of Hitler's army. Around each compound stood a solid wall of grim-faced Germans in full battle order; every few yards two of them crouched behind Slouthern machine guns, and drawn up on the road outside were armoured cars. Literally hundreds of troops were paraded on the roads, each man armed with rifle or Tommy gun and carrying a "spud masher" hand grenade in his belt. The prisoners murmured uneasily; whatever was "up" was obviously very big indeed.

After the count by the *Feldwebel* in charge of each compound, and the inevitable confusion owing partly to inability to count and partly to the propensity of the men to bob about and put him off, a hush fell upon the assembly. Into the R.A.F. compound strode the *Kommandant,* the adjutant, and the official German interpreter. The latter called out:

"You will listen, *ja?*"

"*Ja!*" roared back a thousand throats. This was going to be good, everyone thought. The adjutant fidgeted and told the interpreter to get on with it. That worthy cleared his throat and read from a kind of scroll held up short-sightedly to his eyes.

"The German Government has been always mindful of the duty it owes to its prisoners and the obligations imposed upon it by the terms of the International Agreement signed by it at The Hague in 1926. Therefore it has always shown the utmost clemency toward the enemy when captured and has endeavored to accord them the treatment due to honorably captured prisoners."

Shouts of "Spit it out!" and "In a pig's ear!" interrupted him. He paused uncertainly and was waved on by the now reddening adjutant. The *Kommandant* looked at the sky. He was an elderly man who had been a prisoner himself in the First World War and was often thought to show more sympathy to his charges than most other Germans in the camp. Again the voice proceeded:

"But the German Government was shocked to note that after the recent abortive enemy raid on the seaport of Dieppe, when Canadian troops attempted to invade the continent and were thrown off by the victorious *Wehrmacht,* many Germans soldiers were found shot

in the back, their hands having been tied behind
them."

All the men were quiet now, tense with expectancy.
What was all this leading up to? They exchanged ap-
prehensive glances and looked over at the surrounding
soldiers.

The interpreter shuffled with his papers; then, seeing
the eye of the adjutant on him, hurried to continue.

"Therefore the German Government has no alternative but to register its horror and concern at this
barbarous treatment of its soldiers by making an example not only of the men who perpetrated this terrible
crime but also of the terror gangsters who nightly
bomb the beloved Fatherland and kill hundreds of innocent women and children."

There was a long moment of stunned silence.

Then, "Oh Jesus," breathed someone. "They're going to shoot us."

"In future," bellowed the interpreter, "all members
of the enemy air force and all Canadians of the enemy
army in German hands will have their hands tied from
nine in the morning until nine at night."

He stopped and the watching ranks of German soldiers gripped their guns more menacingly, preparing for
the demonstration they obviously felt was certain to
come: the Britishers would be sure to riot and try to
break out on hearing of this dreadful punishment.
Nothing stirred. Then someone giggled, and in an instant a great wave of laughter had welled up from the
assembled prisoners, laughter that was caught and re-
doubled by the Canadians in their adjacent compound
until it spread throughout the camp, a sea of men roar-
ing themselves silly in relief and at the thought of hundreds of fully-armed Germans mustered for the sole
purpose of tying up a couple of thousand helpless
prisoners. The R.A.F. men rocked with mirth, all except two who, in the noise and movement, seized the
opportunity to knot a miniature Union Jack to the
bayonet of a nearby guard standing engrossed in the
proceedings.

In bewilderment the soldiers looked to their officers for guidance. The little adjutant had flung down his hat and was stamping energetically on it, his swarthy features distorted with rage. Above the volume of laughter his screams were barely heard.

"Tie the pigs up and see how they like that!"

He turned and went to stride out of the compound, accomplishing only a few yards, however, for his inflamed eyes immediately caught sight of the little British flag waving imperiously in the morning breeze on the end of the hapless guard's rifle. The guard was an old man, one of many who had been pressed into service for prison camp duty, and he stared blankly at the officer who was pointing and struggling to catch his breath.

"You damned idiot! Look!"

Terrified, the guard turned to look, the bayonet turning of course with him. His face, as he turned back to confront his stuttering officer, was a study.

"So, you play jokes, eh?"

"Nein, Herr Hauptmann, nein. . . ."

The laughter became insensate. Strong men leaned on each other and wept. Before they were in any condition to notice again what was happening, the *Kommandant* had ordered the flag to be removed and was conducting the adjutant away, talking quietly and firmly.

The day's fun was just starting: it was destined to go down in the history of the prison camps. Ten young German soldiers filed solemnly into the compound, each carrying a stool and heap of string and rope. They seated themselves and prepared for action.

"Now!" yelled the interpreter. "You will all line up and be tied. *Ja?*"

"Ja!" chorused the mob of milling men. Now fully aware that they were immobilizing a great number of German troops, they were determined to protract affairs as long as possible. About two hours later, after much shouting and expostulating on the part of their captors, they were arranged in single file. The team of tiers worked with a will and it took the first prisoners

quite five minutes to remove the string and take their places again at the end of the line.

This continued for the rest of the day. As he was tied up, each man filed around, took off his string in the nearest latrine, and joined the line of prisoners awaiting their turn. At four o'clock, when everyone, including the Germans, was getting hungry and thirsty, a total of about fifty men appeared to be tied up, and the tying team, now weary and hand-sore, had exhausted their supply of string.

Returning to the scene of strife, the adjutant blew up again, bets being laid on the probability of his having a seizure before dark. He ordered the obvious remedy. As soon as a man had been tied up he was set apart in another half of the compound and not allowed to mingle with the untied men. By eight, in failing light, the job was done; everyone had been tied. The adjutant looked at his watch.

"Right!" he commanded. "Untie them now." Rules had to be kept.

The Germans looked at each other expressively and the untying began. This time, in the dark, it was easy. The men quickly armed themselves with pieces of string, and as their hands were untied they walked back to the end of the line, tied themselves up again, and awaited their turn.

At one in the morning the adjutant rebelled.

"Go to hell!" he screamed and stalked out of the gate, followed by roars of laughter. Tired but happy, the prisoners piled back into their huts, eagerly discussing the sole topic of string and how to get more of it. At this rate they could keep all these troops hanging about for weeks.

They did, too. For some weeks the string method was used by the Germans and although it was mighty inconvenient for the Britishers to have their hands tied all day, it was even more so for the Germans. Of course, after the first day's *débâcle* a better system was evolved and eventually chains were used. But so many chains disappeared down the "forty-holer" that the Germans decided to forget the whole thing, and nine months after Dieppe no more was heard of tying or chaining prisoners. It was a triumph for the common man.

4

LAMSDORF

So time went on until a long weary year had been passed at Lamsdorf. A diary kept from day to day would have contained nothing of importance to an outsider, although the activities carried on by the camp seemed to occupy the minds of the inmates well enough. It was during this year that one bright New Zealander, whose father kept a general store, had an idea that was soon to be copied by dozens of men.

In a prison camp there was little money. True, a few of the men, notably army privates who had been out on working parties, scraped together small sums of *Deutsches Lagergeld,* or special camp money, which consisted of little pink slips of paper with the value printed on them in black. But as few possessed this money, its uses were limited, and men who wanted to sell their Red Cross cigarette ration could do so only by contacting someone who had the necessary food or clothing to exchange for it.

To the New Zealander came the momentous notion of opening an exchange mart. Dusty, as he was known, not only filled a long-felt want, but made himself a small fortune in cigarettes during the first two or three weeks, and cigarettes made life considerably easier in a camp such as VIIIB. Not only could they provide many happy hours of smoking but they were an open sesame to extra bread and margarine, bought from the guards, and invaluable for supplying various bodily wants such as toothpaste, brushes and shaving gear. Dusty's little shop in compound three became the

Lloyd's coffee house of its area and many were the bargains obtained over its tea-chest counter. The procedure was simple. The goods one had to sell or exchange were taken to Dusty, who paid either a price in cigarettes, set by a kind of camp stock exchange every week, or for a small charge put them on display for exchange with the goods one required. The two tea chests that served as his shop were placed at the entrance to his particular barrack and soon even the Germans were inspecting his wares and no doubt wishing that they too could spare the price in cigarettes for a pair of shoes or a tin of luncheon meat.

Naturally, competitors were quick to follow Dusty's example and before long every compound had its shops, until the camp committee was compelled to limit them, issuing a license to the lucky ones allowed to remain open. In compound six, referred to as the casbah because of its motley collection of British soldiers from Palestine, Africa and other faraway places, barter flourished. A luminary of the trade was Abdul, an Arab, who had apparently found himself swept up by the advancing *Afrika Korps* in the North African desert and carried protestingly across the sea to a cold and uninviting Europe. He constructed a sort of box consisting of three shelves, and attached to it a length of rope. This he hung from his neck and thus accoutered would parade the barrack huts, calling, "You buy, yes? You buy my nice clothes, shoes, coffee, yes? I get you anything, yes? Anything Sahib." The customer would be treated to an expansive smile and a sweeping bow, before being unmercifully rooked.

Coward joined wholeheartedly into the fun and sometimes almost enjoyed himself when something particularly exciting happened. He regularly produced and took part in prisoners' shows at the converted barrack that served as a theater, occasionally composing catchy tunes himself, and managing prizefights which were a great attraction. But always at the back of his mind was a plan waiting to burst into life. He had explored the possibilities of escape from the camp it-

self and could see that it was futile to try, although the
escape committee had placed his name on their list of
hundreds of men willing to take their turn. Indeed,
there was no alternative. Escape entailed weeks of
careful preparation and was rarely successful. It was
extremely difficult to acquire the necessary civilian
clothing, and continual searches by the *Gestapo* and
the *S.S.* made the storing up of food and maps a chancy
business. The actual escape was of such a nature that
few men ever got through the wire and several met
their deaths in the attempt.

The most popular method was tunneling, and well
the Germans knew it. Dubbed as "ferrets," a platoon of
guards would probe the ground outside the wire with
long steel poles. Too often they were rewarded and
undid the painful work of many months. One party of
men did manage to drive a tunnel clean out under the
wire and into the edge of the forest; over fifty men
went out that way before the "ferrets" discovered the
spot. That night at roll call the men were lectured in a
school-masterly tone by the adjutant, through the
interpreter.

"This will not do," he thundered. "You are children to think you can outwit the resources of the German army so. Even if you do manage to crawl through
your ridiculous tunnels you cannot possibly get back to
Britain, it is too far."

Ironic cheers greeted this advice and his temper began to rise.

"You can laugh," he went on, "but we know of the
existence of all your tunnels. Don't think you can fool
us. This silly business must cease."

Even as he spoke some of the men were scattering
earth down their trousers legs, scraped from a tunnel
in that very compound. This was a favorite method of
disposing of the tell-tale evidence, as it left almost no
trace on the dusty parade ground. After a further
harangue he left to a final rousing cheer. The same
night a plump guard, pounding his beat around the
outer wire, collapsed through the ground as he hit

a tunnel and stood bellowing shoulder-deep in the earth. The adjutant's reflections about this incident were not known.

Another way of trying to get through was less hilarious. To time the swinging searchlights and cut laboriously through the two fences and intervening coils of wire called for a great deal of nerve and immense luck. Only one man was completely successful with this method and he managed it not once, but twice. He was a Pole in the R.A.F. and had been shot down over Hamburg in the summer of 1942. Pieter was his name; a burly pock-marked man of medium height, noted for his impeccable manners and charm. He was a true friend to all who knew him, but if he had one fault it was his intense loathing of anyone or anything German. Constantly he had to be restrained from strangling Germans at night with his bare hands, and could never understand why.

Pieter and an English R.A.F. sergeant one night contrived to cut their way through the wire in a dense fog and bolted for the East. It seemed that their luck was very good and in two nights, traveling on foot, they had arrived at his home town of Lwow where he planned to stay with relations until a contact in the Polish Underground could smuggle them through the country to Stettin. There they would obtain forged papers to take them via Sweden back to Britain. This little plan was foiled, however, when his brother-in-law at Lwow, who happened to work for the German police, informed his employers that two British airmen were sheltering in his house. The pair were promptly captured and escorted back to Lamsdorf, to spend an uncomfortable stretch in the "cooler."

To everyone's surprise, Pieter insisted on making another attempt at the earliest moment, declining this time to allow his friend to accompany him. More baffling, he refused to carry any "papers" or more than a couple of tins of food.

"Only very little will I need, boys," he said. "I'll be coming back very soon."

After several false starts, luck favored him again; he wriggled through the wire one night, avoided the shots from the guards, and vanished in the misty darkness.

The escape committee breathed easier. "Good old Piet. He'll make it this time."

A few days later he was back and serving his time in solitary confinement. On his release from durance vile, a crowd gathered around him. The head of the escape committee caught his arm.

"That was fast, Piet," he said. "I told you to take the proper papers and food with you. You simply couldn't escape home traveling as light as you did."

Pieter looked at him with his eyes dancing, a sure sign that he was happy.

"Escape?" he answered. "I didn't want to escape. I went home all right—to Poland. I wanted to get back to Lwow for a few hours."

"Is that all? What on earth—"

"You see, I had to kill my brother-in-law. It was a matter of honor, if you like. He gave us away on our last trip."

"But you can't just kill a bloke like that. You'd better give up that idea." The Britisher was firm. "No more larks now, Piet."

Pieter grinned. "No, no more larks. I've done what I went to do. Strangled him outside his own door and buried his rotten body in the woods. No one will ever find out."

Sure enough, he had. Surrendering himself to the police, he had returned to a twenty-one day sentence in the cells, leaving his brother-in-law beneath the leaves of a Polish redoubt. Pieter was a good friend, but no one crossed him and lived to boast about it.

Occasionally men discussed the possibility of escaping by vaulting the wire with a long pole, but as far as Coward recalls this was never successful. The vaulter, even in darkness, would be an unmistakable target for the guards in the postern boxes when he crashed on the other side, besides the risk involved in breaking a limb or even his neck. One man did try a particularly horrible form of escape and nearly died in the attempt.

The latrines provided for each compound had earned the title of "forty-holers" because of the four banks of seats, ten to a side, that occupied the low draughty building in which they were housed. The sewage from each "forty-holer" ran down into a noisome cesspit behind the building, and it was the job of one of the Russians to empty the contents of the pit every week into an enormous barrel on wheels. The pit was the receptacle for anything that the men wished to get rid of without the Germans knowing. Many a German "stool pigeon" had come to an untimely end and his dismembered body dropped into the pit, never to be seen again. The actions of the miserable Russian with his dripping bucket did no more than stir up the mass putrescence so that the stench filled the camp, turning all stomachs, no matter how hardened. The barrel was duly filled through a hole at the top and then the contraption was pulled by a horse through the camp and out of the front gate to a field about a mile away.

The prisoner in question had conceived the unhappy notion of stowing himself inside the barrel and once clear of the gates to make a clean break. Getting in was easy enough; he had only to bribe the Russian with a packet of cigarettes not to fill the barrel up. The poor fellow lowered himself through the hole on top and the lid was fastened down above him. Then began the worst journey that surely any man has made. Although the barrel was partly filled, there was enough sewage to make the atmosphere unbearable, and he began to gasp for breath before the cart had covered a hundred yards. As the cart trundled through the gates a weak voice was heard crying for help, and the guards found inside the barrel a sorry specimen indeed. The fumes had well nigh killed the man and he collapsed on the ground in a condition that can be imagined.

The best way to leave camp was obviously to go out on a working-party, as Coward soon discovered. The parties were usually sent to smaller and more lightly guarded camps, and now and again to farms where it

was easy to slip away. Under international law only
army privates could be detailed for work, and the
work was supposed to have no connection with the war
effort, though whether that could ever be so is a moot
point. N.C.O.s could volunteer, and many did, so that
they could take nominal charge of a party and represent the men's interests. It needed someone with au-
thority to look after a group of men who had no rank
themselves, and the Germans would recognize no sug-
gestions or complaints unless they came from an
N.C.O. Quite apart from the opportunities to escape,
working parties usually gave plenty of scope for sabotage. Very many ex-prisoners of Lamsdorf will remember the exploits of such men as Duke Boyle, Bill Clem-
son, Billy Tuft, Johnny Vigors and Harry Botton, who
were not labeled "trouble makers" by the Germans
without ample reason.

Coward duly entered his name on the volunteer list
for working and after a period of weeks was told
to report to the *Arbeitslager,* the compound in which
all men coming in or going out on jobs bunked down.
Here he learned from the *Arbeitsführer,* a sad-

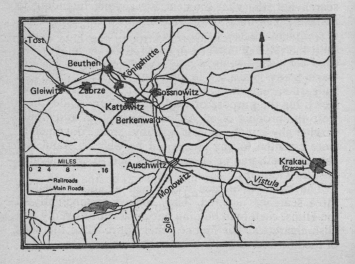

looking *Feldwebel,* that he was to take charge of a party detailed to work at a wood mill. He introduced himself to the lads and asked them if they knew anything about the place.

"It's a small place about forty miles off at a village called Tost," said one, lighting a cigarette. "A pal of mine has just come back from there. Seems a decent place. Bags of grub, anyway."

Coward turned to him quickly.

"Look here, chum, a decent place is where we work hard for the Jerries. That's why it stays decent. The sooner was can muck up that side of it, the better. What d'you say, blokes?" he appealed to the others lounging around. "Come on, let's hear what you think. Do we slave our guts for Hitler or do we make as much hell as we can out of this wood mill?"

There were grins.

"Save your breath, cobber," said a lanky Australian. "Too flippin' right we'll make hell out of the place."

Coward laughed. "That's the style, lads. Take plenty of matches with you, then. They're always handy."

A few days later the party were ordered into the search hut, the vital moment for anyone intending to make a break later. Concealed in Coward's kit bag was a complete escape outfit, manufactured by the committee and its numerous band of helpers. It included dyed army clothes for use as civilian gear, and a set of travel passes made out in the name of "Karl Joseph," a Bulgarian, entitling him to travel anywhere in the Reich for the purpose of work. Beautifully made, these were the product of an Australian corporal and would survive any but the closest scrutiny. Such "documents" were essential to any escaper, if he were to stand any chance at all, and at all costs they had to be smuggled past the Germans.

The twenty-five men were lined against a wall as three searchers entered. They looked nonchalantly at the Huns, each man holding out a packet of twenty English cigarettes. The first searcher approached the head of the line and smiled humorlessly.

"Give," he grunted. The cigarettes were passed to him, but the expected result was not forthcoming. "Open up," he said, pointing to the man's kit bag and box.

"You dirty bastard," exclaimed the offended one, a diminutive Scot. "Taking ma fags and searching me too. You—" For an answer the guard spat neatly into his face and then stood back as Coward and the rest of the men struggled to restrain Jock from hurling himself at the grinning German.

"Can it, you fool," jerked Digger, the Ausie. "That sort of rough stuff will only get you a bullet. Leave the swine to the boys—they'll take care of him later."

The wrathful Scot swallowed his anger and submitted to having his bags searched. Several camp-made compasses and maps were unearthed, together with a hundred or so bars of soap, useful currency in the outside world of Germany where the soap issued to civilians was concocted of pumice powder and horse fat. The searchers murmured their satisfaction and applied themselves to their work with added zest.

As officer in charge, Coward was left until last. His brain raced to find an idea as the searchers moved slowly toward him, a pile of prohibited articles growing in size behind them. When each man had been cleared, he was made to stand by the door, and here Coward saw his chance. Gabbling as fast as possible, in case any of the guards understood English well, he called to the Scot across the room.

"Jockyousonofabitch, throw a fit will you, for Chrissake."

Catching the words, Jock straightway obeyed, swaying violently and crumpling into a heap on the floor. With a cry, Coward sprang forward and knelt beside the moaning Scot, taking his kit bag with him.

"*Weg, weg,*" bawled the Germans. "Get back, English pig."

"Keep your wool on," Coward muttered. "Only wanted to help him."

He returned to his place, taking Jock's kit bag with him and leaving his own by the casualty. In a few minutes he had been proclaimed free of any suspect material and was helping his friend to his feet.

"Thanks, pal," he breathed. "Talk about blinkin' Scotch mist!"

They marched down a lane outside the camp and for the first time in a year Coward saw and smelt the outside world. It was wonderful to see the trees close at hand again and to walk in the stubbly grass beside the track. A child passed them, staring wide-eyed at the prisoners, and Coward threw her a piece of chocolate. He was filled with a sense of freedom and well-being, optimistically bidding Lamsdorf farewell. Presently they reached the railway station, and, wonder of wonders, were ushered into a train compartment equipped with seats. Ten severe guards accompanied them, and as soon as the train began to move the game commenced of distracting their attention while some of the men undid every screw within reach with bits of tin or any other possible implements. It was not much to do, but every bit helped.

They had been traveling some little time when Coward noticed what appeared to be a great fire burning in the distance; as they drew nearer it grew into a thick black pall of smoke that seemed to be pouring from a cluster of chimneys set among trees bordering a river. There was a nauseous odor which puzzled Coward until suddenly it struck him where he had smelt it before. In France during the big German push, when an R.A.F. plane had crashed near his gun emplacement, they had run to help. The flames engulfing the wreck had shriveled the pilot to a crisp and driven them back coughing, but not before the distinctive, sweetish smell of burning flesh had caught their throats.

Coward looked meditatively at the chimneys as they slowly passed and fell behind the speeding train. He leaned over and spoke to the guard opposite.

"What is that?" He pointed. "Where—what name?"

The guard stared at him impassively, then shrugged.

"Auschwitz," he said.

"Here, you blokes," Coward called to the others. "Anyone heard of Auschwitz?"

"You can search me, Charlie," replied Digger. "Why, what do they do there?"

"I don't know," said Coward quietly. "That's just what I was wondering."

5

SABOTAGE

Tost proved to be nothing but a collection of little houses nestling in the corner of a great forest, the same spread of trees that stretched to Oppeln in the northwest and Breslau in the north, covering a tremendous area of southern Germany and Poland.

The little party of men straggled down the one and only street of the village, waiting for a sight of the working camp. But they were marched some way farther and eventually came to the camp about half a mile off the rough road. It was a wood mill right enough, feeding itself on the surrounding forest. A gaunt wooden machinery house stood next to a low and extensive building that was evidently a log store, for outside it were stacked huge piles of timber, ready for the saw.

A stocky South African, whose name Coward had learned was Jack Barney, gave him an excited nudge.

"You boys won't ask for a guy to be put on top of that lot, will you? Will that heap burn!"

Coward clucked a reproving tongue.

"Dear me, corporal," he remonstrated. "I trust you have no ideas about burning yonder pile of firewood. That wouldn't be nice. Think of Uncle Adolf and what he would say if all his nice timber caught alight."

"Come orf it," muttered Joe, walking on the other side. "If that bleedin' place is still standing this time next week, I'm a ruddy Jerry meself."

They filed in at the gate in the wire, Coward noting with approval that only a single height of it stood between them and freedom. His spirits rose yet higher.

"Once aboard the lugger," he said to himself, "and you're away, Charlie boy."

The living quarters were to the familiar pattern, a wooden hut standing in the corner of a compound, and an eager inspection revealed a filthy hovel showing little improvement on the conditions back in Lamsdorf. Disappointed but not disheartened, the men knew they would soon be able to lick it into shape and clean up some of the dirt.

They soon settled down at Tost. The German in charge was a rednosed *Unteroffizier* who seemed to enjoy life as much as the limited resources allowed. He was a fairly cheerful soul and it almost—but not quite—cut the men to the heart to think how he was to suffer in the very near future. Their work consisted of hauling the logs up a sloping ramp to the top storie of the small factory and slicing them into planks with a circular saw. The planks were then slid down into the store below, ready for lorries from the nearest town. By this time the hot airless summer of middle Europe was well into its stride. In the bright sunshine the men worked happily and for a few days the *Unteroffizier* and his modest staff of Germans were very pleased with them. Then a peculiar thing came to light. The more these men worked, the less appeared to be accomplished; even less was done than when the half-starved Jews had been working at the mill. The *Unteroffizier* was worried and spoke to Coward about it.

"Look," he growled in passable English and jabbing with his pipe; this was his inseparable companion, a fact not unnoticed by Coward. "Look, Mr. Coward. Your men they work hard, *ja*, very hard, but those planks they never come down to the lorries. Why is that, eh?"

Coward looked appropriately sympathetic. "I'll go and have a word with them," he assured him. "We can't have production held up, can we?"

He walked off and climbed the stairs to where a drowsy guard dozed in the heat outside the door of the factory. Inside was a hive of industry, but the mystery of the nonappearing planks was quickly solved. All the logs that had been pulled up the ramp during the last day were now sawn up into long slats and nailed together, making a long ladder. It would be the work of a moment to fit the lengths together and slip it over the wire.

"Quiet, blokes," called Coward. "Old muckface downstairs is worried about his bloody planks—the trucks are waiting. It's time we did something about it. Got the petrol, Jack?"

"Sure, Charlie boy."

"Right. I'll go down, then, and maneuver the old bar steward into position. Make it good."

He ran down the stairs and Plan A, as previously worked out, swing into action.

"Oh, *Unteroffizier*," he bawled. "Come here a minute."

He waved the German over to his side until they both stood outside the huge wood store, beneath the tons of dry logs.

"Can you get your lorry under the chute? There's a load to come."

"*Ach,* so? *Gut, gut.*" The German bellowed an order to a driver standing by his machine at the gate. The truck backed around and pulled up under the chute. Coward thought, and hoped, that he could detect a smell of petrol other than that from the machine; by now Jack Barney should have liberally doused the wood piles in petrol, in particular soaking the timber stacked alongside the German. Coward held his breath, waiting for the next and final phase. Then, true to form, as he did twenty times a day, the *Unteroffizier* produced a matchbox, contentedly puffed at his pipe, and tossed away the match. As he did so, Jack also struck a match and plunged it into the pool of petrol.

It happened. With a roar a sheet of flame shot up the stacks of timber, showering sparks. Coward cannoned into the astounded *Unteroffizier* sending him reeling.

"Quick," he shouted. "The wood's alight."

The remark was somewhat obvious; in a matter of seconds the store was ablaze from end to end. The

Germans ran frantically around it, bellowing. Most unaccountably, the petrol tank of the truck had also burst into flame before the driver could move the machine to safety. The *Unteroffizier* sprinted to a telephone, knowing in his despair that the nearest fire brigade was over ten miles away and not very good at that.

"Come on, lads, lend a hand here," shouted Coward. "Do your worst—don't let a blasted inch survive."

The Britishers swarmed about, ostensibly falling over themselves in their concern to fight the fire, but to such little effect that the flames spread rapidly until they engulfed the factory itself and threatened the house near the gate in which the Germans lived. This consummation was assisted by Jack, who disappeared in the general confusion and expended his last pint of petrol in the back room that was used as a kitchen. Digger employed himself in hurling manageable logs into the fire; he explained to an indignant guard that he was choking it. After several minutes the *Unteroffizier* reappeared in a flaming temper to watch the scene and superintend the firefighting.

"*Verflucht,* over here. Bring the fire buckets, *schnell!*" he shrieked to the Britishers. Alas, the buckets were empty. "Quick, the beaters," he implored. But the brush-beaters had long since been added to the flames. He gave up and sat moaning with his head in his hands, obviously trying to prepare a story for the authorities.

Some time later the fire brigade arrived, pouring water on to the smouldering ruins. The one place that had survived the blaze was the living hut of the prisoners themselves. Coward went over to the *Unteroffizier*.

"Look here," he began, "I hope you don't think we had anything to do with this packet. Everyone saw you throw that match into the wood."

"Hush," muttered the *Unteroffizier,* only too aware of how the fire started, or so he thought. "It was accident. The sun and the wood—so hot—combustion."

"Combustion my backside," snorted Coward. "You set it alight, cock. I'd hate to be in your shoes." The

German groaned. "This means big trouble for you, doesn't it? Still, you're a good sort—we'll say nothing. That is, if you'll do us a favor or two in return."

The German looked at him stupidly. "How—what? You wouldn't tell anyone, would you? What do you want?"

"Well, a bit of freedom for a start. We could ask you to get some blank traveling passes for us—" Alarm showed in the German's eyes. "—but we won't." Followed by instant relief. "Let us walk down to the village if we like and buy things at the shops. What about it? You're a good sort. We don't want to mention anything to your officer unless you make us. It'd upset us to think of you on the Russian front."

"*Jawohl,*" stuttered the unhappy man. "You can go out—but no escapes, eh?"

Coward was shocked. "Of course not," he protested. But as he walked away he knew that he had won and that the way was clear for his big bid. It had been a grand day's work and he was well satisfied. His only regret was that the ladder so laboriously constructed had perished forgotten in the flames.

A celebration was called for in the hut that night. Under the dull glow of two electric lamps all the Britishers gathered around while Coward gave them a little talk.

"Well, lads, we've enjoyed ourselves today and practically stopped production at this place. We can say we've earned our pay that's mounting up back home. Now, the *Unteroffizier* has got the fear of God in him over this business, but we shall have to watch him. He says we can walk to the village but be careful when you do in case his blokes turn nasty and take a pot shot at you, on the pretence that you're escaping. Go down by all means, but don't antagonize him too far. He believes we know he started the fire and would be only too glad to get his own back on us. Tomorrow he'll most likely get some makeshift machinery working for us, but go easy for a bit until we can see another fool-proof way of mucking things up. As you

know, Jack Barney, Walter Connolly, Pilski and myself are hoping to make a break soon, so until then be
reasonably good boys and keep your noses clean. After
we go you can blow the place up for all I care."

There was a subdued cheer and Connolly man-
handled forward a small barrel of light beer which had
been liberated earlier from the guards' house. "Bring
out your mugs, gents," he called, "and let's have your
orders." Skillfully fashioned from empty cans that had
contained peas or condensed milk, with handles fitted
on by means of tin clips, the mugs were surprisingly ef-
ficient, and the men smacked their lips appreciatively
over the drinks. The evening passed peacefully with
little noise. The four escapers sat on Coward's bunk
and discussed their plans, while around them crouched
several helpers engaged in making compasses from razor blades and copying the map in his escape gear on
to linen handkerchiefs.

The next day a small generator arrived from the village to power the saw, and while some of the men were
set to work clearing up the ashes of the mill and re-
pairing the guards' house, others resumed the cutting
of the logs into planks under the vigilant watch of a
reinforced guard. Several German officers came and
went, staring suspiciously at the prisoners although it
was clear that the *Unteroffizier* had exonerated them
from all blame, knowing that their combined testimony
would incriminate him.

In the early evening Coward and Barney took a walk
to the village, taking care to remain in full view for as
long as possible. Word had reached them of a civil in-
ternment camp in the vicinity, and to Coward this
spelled a chance to barter his escape clothes, crudely
dyed with the red jam issued at Lamsdorf, for something more presentable. Barney was ill-equipped with
clothes, and as for Connolly and Pilski the Pole, they
possessed only the shabby remnants of uniform they
stood up in.

A short tramp brought the two to the barbed wire
and brick buildings of quite a large camp. A number

of civilians standing about inside grinned in curiosity at the pair of British soldiers strolling up the road. Presently they were near enough to talk.

"Who in God's name are you?" asked a bearded gentleman who bore a remarkable resemblance to an orchestral conductor of fame in England.

Coward enlightened him. "We want some civilian clothes," he added, "and we'd be very grateful if you could help us."

"Well I'm damned," said the Beard. Although probably a Slav, his English was effortless. "If you stand there what you will get are a couple of bullets. Our protectors are most sensitive about social visits. Quick now, hurry around to the back and wait by a tree you'll find near the wire. We can talk there."

The two made a cautious detour and found a reception committee of some twenty inmates awaiting them. Questions, a mixture of many tongues freely illustrated with emphatic gestures and signs, plied back and forth. The civilians were anxious for news of the war, but the Britishers could only tell them of the B.B.C. bulletins received before they left Lamsdorf.

"Look," said the Beard, whose name it now appeared was Rakowski, a journalist, "it is impossible to get anything over the wire to you. You must go to the village grocery shop and ask for Rudy. He is a German boy who comes into this camp every day to work in the kitchen. He brings us what he can and he will help you, too." He waved them away. "I advise you to be off now; it is dangerous here. I will give Rudy some trousers for you. I hope they fit. Au revoir, and good luck, gentlemen."

They slipped through a copse and regained the road.

"Blimey, that was a bit of all right," said Coward.

"Old Santa Claus sounded straight enough," replied Barney, "but let's wait till we meet this Rudy character before we count our chicks. He might dish us, don't forget."

The grocery shop, being the only one, was not hard to discover. In its gloomy interior a portly *frau* waited

behind the single counter; she recoiled at the sight of
the prisoners' uniforms. For a moment the unaccustomed smells of every small general shop swept Coward back several years; it was an effort to gather himself together and offer his hand with a smile.

"Friends," he said hopefully. "Mr. Rakowski,
Rudy."

The woman did not take his hand, but walked
quickly to the door and looked outside. Then she
turned and smiled uncertainly.

"Rudy," repeated Coward. "Where is Rudy?"

"Rudy? *Ja, ja. Ein Moment, bitte.*"

She disappeared into the shop parlor and came out
with a boy about twelve years old, an impudent-look-
ing youngster with ruddy cheeks and an excited grin.

Coward wasted no time. "Here," he called, and
pressed a bar of chocolate into the boy's willing hands.
"You work in *lager—Herr Rakowski—ja?*" The boy
nodded. "You bring tomorrow—er, *morgen früh*
—clothes," he shook his uniform, "from Rakowski to
me." He jabbed at himself, "here. Understand?"

"*Ja, ja,*" said the boy eagerly. "I speak small English, Herr Rakowski tell English me."

"That's the boy," said Coward. "You bring one parcel here, tomorrow. Good lad." He patted the boy's
shoulder while the mother looked on nervously.

"*Schokolade?*"

"*Ja,* much *schokolade.* Lots of *schokolade* for you,
son. Tomorrow, here, okay?"

"Okay," returned the boy proudly.

They thanked the woman and left the shop.

"We're in clover, Jacko," said Coward. "You've just
got to know how to handle these people."

"Like hell," said Barney. "How d'you know he or
his mother won't go straight to the Jerries?"

"And lose his job at the camp, with the perks from
the prisoners? Act your age, Jack. Anyway, he won't
split. Kids like chocolate too much and in Germany
they hardly know what it is. Come to think of it, if we
swap our fags for some of the other lads' chocolate, we

might be able to buy some cake biscuits from the shop. Look pretty hard tack, but they're just what we want."

"Oh sure," said Barney. "I daresay if we give the nearest station master a tin of beans he'll lay on a special train for us."

"What's the matter with you, all of a sudden? When everything's coming our way you're like a blessed Jonah."

"Listen, Charlie," said Barney with quiet intensity, "I'm in this as much as you are, and where I come from we usually get what we set out for. I just don't believe in acting like a bloody bull at a gate. You take too many chances. Later on, when we have to take 'em, I'll be right in there with you. But where's the sense in risking the whole show before we've begun?"

"I'm a gambler. If you don't take chances—"

"Gambler my aunt fanny. What about me and the others—you gambling for us too?"

"Well, someone's got to organize the thing."

"Fat chance anyone else has of doing it."

"Oh, stuff it. Come on, we're just in time for pay."

The weekly pay at the camp consisted of about twelve *Lagermarken,* or camp marks, and with it they were able to buy such things as razor blades and pencils. In most working parties a man was usually allowed out with a guard to make these purchases at the nearest village shops, but in the present circumstances the *Unteroffizier* could not help permitting any of them to stroll as they pleased in the evening.

When work was finished the following day, Coward informed the Germans that he was going to visit the village and walked down to the shop, his heart beating heavily. As he entered, the boy came out of the inner room and held up a large bundle of clothing.

"Good boy, Rudy," said Coward, passing over three more bars of chocolate. He knocked on the door of the parlor, found the room empty, and went in. As quickly as he could, he stripped off his uniform, put on the rather small but mercifully not too tight civilian suit which he found in the bundle, and donned the uniform again over it. There was a clump of boots outside as two German guards came into the shop and stood chatting with Rudy for a couple of minutes. Coward let them get clear, then, feeling like a trussed chicken, emerged, promised the boy further rewards for more clothes, and slipped away. Once in the safety of the camp hut, the suit was stuffed up the chimney of the stove.

The procedure was repeated without incident on several successive nights until all four escapers had clothes of some sort, though the picture they presented raised a good deal of ribald laughter. Coward filled his amply. Barney looked the smartest in a double-breasted serge suit that was definitely nearing the end of its useful life but would serve very nicely for the task at hand. Pilski the Pole, a tailor before the war, sported a combination of dungarees and cunningly disguised uniform, looking like something between a soldier and a chimney-sweep. Connolly's suit proved to be unwearable, having been made for a man half his size, so it was donated to the hut for future occasions and the resourceful Liverpool man, with the assistance of Pilski, dyed his uniform a light brown with the strainings of boiled jam and sewed on bone buttons filched from the guards' house.

Coward scribbled a note of thanks to be delivered to Rudy and thence to Rakowski and his fellows, and the four settled down to complete their plans. The party was to split into two pairs and make for the town of Gleiwitz. From there, if their luck held, a train could be caught for Dresden. At Dresden a change of trains to one proceeding to Ulm, about eighty kilometers from the Swiss border on Lake Constance. The last leg would be walked, as all trains approaching a neutral border were closely inspected at each station. It was considered that the best point at which to slip across was near Schauffhausen, where the frontier was not so heavily guarded as it was farther down toward Basle.

As darkness fell on the appointed day, each man

made his preparations, his pockets filled with bread, sausage and whatever food he had saved from his Red Cross parcels. Each had a rough map of the route and as much German currency as he could gather. Coward had estimated the fares needed for rail travel and had drawn from the escape committee at Lamsdorf enough to cover four or five persons.

"Everyone ready?" asked Coward, doing his best to keep the tenseness he felt out of his voice. "All got your compass in your pocket and your maps okay?" They slipped their small packs on to their shoulders.

"All ready. Let's go," said Connolly. His quiet demeanor never faltered; the demands of prison life had brought him an imperturbability that nothing, not even this, could shake.

"Right you blokes," Coward addressed the men who were staying behind, "give us time to get over to the wire and then you can start."

"And make it good, you bunch of ugly drips," added Barney, "or I'll personally do the lot of you."

"Good luck," called out Joe. "See you in the Rose and Crown, Charlie."

"That's a date, nosher. Come on, then, and keep your heads down."

The four left the hut and ran swiftly to the other side of the compound, bending low in the darkness. Almost immediately, a terrific din broke out in the hut behind them, punctuated with shouts of anger and loud crashes. Coward grinned at the performance. The row increased in volume and ferocity, and presently they heard the guards running around the wire and making for the gate. A few moments later the Germans had crashed into the hut, bawling above the noise for the men to quiet down and stop fighting.

Flat on their stomachs, the four began to cut the wire, using pliers they had stolen from the workshop during the fire. Working with the speed of desperation, they bent back the strands and wriggled through. Running blindly into the darkness, stumbling over the uneven ground, they sprinted on until all sounds of the rumpus in camp had vanished. Then Coward called a brief halt for a breather.

"We made it," panted Connolly.

"Now it's up to us," said Barney. "Let's start hoofing it."

"Gleiwitz," breathed Coward, "here we come!"

6

ON THE LOOSE

By the time they reached the road their eyes were becoming accustomed to the dark. Setting their faces southeast they started on the walk to Gleiwitz, where, if all went well, they might be able to jump a train for Dresden. The night was sharp and Coward set a brisk pace.

"As soon as we've got a bit more ground between us and camp," he said, keeping his voice low, "we'd better leave the road, two on each side, and keep parallel with it along the fields."

"That's tricky," replied Barney. "Don't forget the marshes around here. It's better to get to the station as fast as we can before the police are alerted."

"Well, I'm a Dutchman," Coward exclaimed. "That was my idea, but you bellyached so much the other day about taking unnecessary risks—"

"It's the lesser risk of the two, you ape."

"Quiet, you two!" hissed Connolly. "Listen."

The sound of a motorcycle was approaching them fast; the next moment its shaded headlamp beam had swept around a bend in the road ahead. They scrambled for the ditch, but a squeal of brakes as the machine passed told them they had been seen. A voice shouted vociferously in German, then with a roar the machine accelerated on its way again.

"That's done it!"

Cursing, the men climbed back on to the road.

"Of all the rotten, stinking luck—"

"No good moaning," said Coward. "It's best foot

first now. As soon as trouble starts, break for the fields, head for Gleiwitz."

They quickened to a steady jog-trot, their boots seeming to make enough noise on the rough road to rouse the whole countryside. Pilski was the first to hear, after several minutes, the warning note of a truck being driven at speed.

"Come on—into the field!"

They leapt blindly into the ditch, fortunately dry, and were scrambling up the far side when lights appeared along the road. Coward doubled across the springy turf, skidding and sliding, closely followed by Connolly. The first shot rang out, the bullet seeming to sing uncomfortably near them. Then a crackle of several shots, and a shout, sounding like Barney's voice. Coward changed course, sprinting madly; he stole a quick look over his shoulder, yet could discern no one in pursuit, only the gleam of torches from the road and the sudden flashes of rifle fire.

Frenziedly the two leaped over what appeared to be low, single-strand fences in the grass, spotting them just in time to clear them in their stride. There were a number of these and the effort of dancing madly over them winded the two considerably. Reaching a fence of wire net, they hauled themselves painfully over it, catching their hands and clothes, and dropped down on the other side. Coward made for some trees and halted abruptly to fight for breath.

"Christ," he gasped. "The bastards won't chase us."

As he spoke a bullet cut into the undergrowth some distance away. But Connolly was gaping past him.

"Wait a bit," he croaked. "Look at that." Coward turned and could dimly make out a notice board, headed with the bold sign *Verboten,* standing shadowy on the fringe of the trees. "It says something about twenty thousand volts being in that field."

"Holy smoke, the electricity supply for the railway."

"Yes, and us hopping over the cables like a couple of crazy coons. If we'd touched one—"

"Well, we didn't," said Coward. "We'd better look lively. The Jerries are sure to be making a detour around this field."

He wiped the sweat from his face, which had not been produced entirely by the running, and set off in the direction in which he judged the railway lay. In a few minutes they hit it, scaled a fence bordering the permanent way, and stood for a moment listening for sounds of pursuit. All was quiet.

"Where the hell are they?" whispered Connolly.

"Not far away, you can bet your life. Looks as if Jack and Pilski have copped it. All we can do is follow the line along to Gleiwitz as fast as we can."

"The station's bound to have been alerted by now."

"I know, but we can see how things look there—if we can grab a train it'll save us hours. Come on and for God's sake keep your voice down."

Striding from sleeper to sleeper, afraid to attempt to run because of the risk of a twisted ankle, they made their way along the track, seeming to make painfully slow progress, until the dim shapes of a signal box and level crossing gate loomed ahead.

"Dead quiet now," breathed Coward. "We'll hop over the fence again and get back on to the road. Be a lot quicker than this lark."

"Okay, Charlie, but it's a bloody big risk."

"We've got to face that. If we don't make better time than this we're sunk anyway."

Regaining the road, they began a gentle trot again, keeping near enough to the ditch to be able to dive into it whenever sounds of approaching vehicles were heard. Several dispatch riders and cars full of soldiers passed them, traveling at speed in the direction of Gleiwitz. After the umpteenth scramble for cover, Coward optimistically brushed in the darkness at the mud on his suit and declared:

"It's no go, Wally. They're obviously forming up a cordon ahead. We'll have to strike across country and make for Kattowitz instead. They're probably expecting us to break due north toward Stettin, or southwest toward Switzerland, so perhaps it'll put 'em off a bit if we turn away east."

"I'm with you," returned Connolly. "Only for the love of old apples let's get off this flippin' road."

In the light of a very pale and watery moon, he consulted his razorblade compass mounted in a matchbox and a map taken from the top of his small pack. They set off to trudge across the fields, following as far as they could the line of bushes and hedgerows, and hoping thereby to avoid marshland. Once they heard distant shouts and the barking of dogs, but the clamor soon died down, leaving no sounds but their own labored breathing and the sigh of the wind across the flat countryside. Throughout the night they walked, not daring to rest, frequently slipping in the damp earth of a ploughed field or tripping over a bramble. They seemed alone in the world, yet hounded by invisible pursuers; making all speed they could, yet getting nowhere. The first cold light of dawn was streaking the sky when they struck a narrow twisting road which, if they had identified correctly on the map, should lead them straight to Kattowitz.

Coward's relief was immense. "We'd better hole up for the day," he suggested. "I'm just about bushed. Let's just see what's around the corner up here and find a hideout."

But what was around the corner revealed itself at that moment, in the shape of generously proportioned policeman wheeling a bicycle and enjoying an early morning cigarette. The two Britishers stood rooted in their tracks; then Coward muttered "Keep right on." They continued walking, aware of the curious stare fixed on them.

"*Morgen,*" Connolly essayed, nodding affably as they made to pass.

"Just a minute," growled the policeman in German. "Who are you two? What are you up to at this time of the morning?"

Coward turned to his companion, giving an exaggerated shrug of noncomprehension.

"Bluff it out," he said quickly. "If we have to, I'll hit him in the belly, you jump him from behind."

Connolly faced the policeman with startled innocence.

"Excuse us, sir," he managed in halting and atrocious German, "we go to stay with friends in Kattowitz and have walked from the last village to save the fare."

"Ja, ja. But what was that language this fellow was speaking just now? It's not Polish, and yet—"

"Polish!" snorted Connolly. He spat indignantly.

The policeman chuckled. "What are you then?"

"Bulgarians. We work in the mines back there."

"Ach so? Good job?"

Connolly spread his hands expressively. "We work hard. Now is a holiday, so we come to see old friends." He fished in his pocket. "You wish to see our papers?"

"Ja, I'd better. A formality, of course."

They handed over their passes and identity cards. Coward held his breath, remembering how laboriously they had been manufactured at Lamsdorf. The policeman glanced at the Bulgarian eagles at the top of the cards, then returned them with a smile.

"Sehr gut," he grunted. "Keep straight on for Kattowitz. It's only four kilometers—you can't miss it."

With thanks that were certainly sincere, they left him, heaving a sigh as they rounded the bend in the road and were lost to his sight.

"That was close," said Coward in an undertone. "Lucky you can rattle off the lingo a bit, Wally."

"I surprised myself," laughed Connolly. "Anyway, as we were foreigners it served well enough. Now for a good sleep until tonight."

"Better get well away from the road in case he comes back on his beat."

On the far side of a broad field they found a small covert where they burrowed into the bushes and heaped together some dried leaves and twigs for beds.

"So far, so good," said Coward, munching biscuits and cheese from his pack. "We'll have to keep our eyes skinned at Kattowitz, though. They've probably had an alarm by now."

In a few minutes they were both sleeping soundly. The afternoon sun was low in the sky before they roused, stretched their cramped limbs, and chewed a few more biscuits.

"By hokey," groaned Connolly, "what wouldn't I do for a cup of char right now."

"We might be able to get one at the station. We're bound to have to wait hours for a train. Let's get moving."

Cleaning themselves was not easy, but they managed to brush off the worst of the dirt, and once more trod the road.

"Wouldn't mind a shave," remarked Connolly. "We look like a couple of escaped convicts."

"Well, what do you think we are, you silly clot?"

"Still, most of the civvies around here seem to object to shaving. Gives us a bit of local color."

"Shut up and keep quiet."

Dusk was falling as they entered the outskirts of Kattowitz. It was a small and unremarkable mining town, gloomy and unfriendly, and the railway station presented itself like an ancient hat box illuminated with flickering gas lamps. Coward nudged his friend and stepped boldly into the entrance hall. Immediately several faces turned to them and in horror they recognized the uniforms of *SS* men and the *Gestapo*. With the quicker presence of mind, Connolly grabbed Coward's arm and bundled him toward the bright lights and steamy windows of a buffet. Without hesitation he marched up to the counter inside and asked in his own brand of German for two plates of soup. The weary woman ladling out the insipid dish appeared to accept this strange accent as quite usual; she handed over the plates, together with two cups of ersatz coffee. Connolly paid, and they repaired to a table in the corner. In haste they gobbled the meal, the unsavory soup and the burned acorns of the coffee tasting wonderful to their parched throats, and revived their willing spirits.

Coward took a cautious look around him, then leaned across the table and spoke in a whisper.

"We'll have to chance it in a minute. I reckon those blokes out there will be on duty all night. We can't stay in here too long and we can't very well walk out of the station either. So we'll have to take a chance and try to book a ticket."

"Well, if we're going, let's get it over," replied Connolly rising to his feet.

They walked slowly out of the buffet and into the hall. In front of them glowed the window of the booking office; within that small space lay the tickets for home if only they had the luck to get them.

"Here goes," whispered Coward. Pulling out his money he strode up to the window. A face appeared, feminine, blank and impersonal.

"Ja?" it asked.

"Zwei Karten, Dresden," said Coward, hoping that the shaking of his hand was not too noticeable.

Without a flicker, the woman reached for the precious tickets, date-stamped them, and tossed them under the window, reaching at the same time for his money. Impassively, she counted out the change, a small heap of dirty notes and aluminum coins.

"Danke," he muttered and gathered up the pile. Rejoining his companion, he read the excitement in the other's eyes and tried desperately to keep it out of his own face. Together they approached the barrier, looking everywhere but at the the two tall SS men, resplendent in their green and silver coats with each movement tinkling the necklet insignia of their regiment, who stood beside the collector. To themselves, ill-dressed and grimy, the prisoners seemed the object of everyone's attention. Coward felt himself begin to tremble. He handed over the tickets to be punched and immediately one of the SS men demanded passes. The forged documents were produced and, while the Britishers waited with thumping hearts, were carefully scrutinized. Then, miraculously, they were waved on. Trying not to hurry, they made their way to a timetable board and deciphered that the next train to Dresden was not until the early morning.

"Another four and half hours," murmured Coward. "Hell, what can we do in this god-forsaken place?"

"What everyone else has to do—wait and wait and wait," replied Connolly cheerfully. "We got past those two morons all right, Chas, so perhaps our luck's in."

Making themselves as comfortable as possible on a pile of mailbags, they prepared to while away the hours. Several trains came in and departed during the long wait, clearing the platform almost completely of travelers, but it had turned five o'clock before the Dresden train eventually grunted and groaned its way into the station and the two men climbed wearily aboard. They found an empty third-class compartment and composed themselves on the hard wooden seats provided by the *Reichbahn* for the comfort of its passengers.

Hour after hour passed. At every major station the *SS* boarded the train and demanded to see all passes: it was a torture of suspense that the Britishers could not avoid. At Breslau two fussy little German women entered the compartment and unwittingly helped matters along by mislaying their identity cards and taking so long to find them in their baggage that the *SS* gave up in despair and only had time for a cursory inspection of the forged Bulgarian passes.

By the time Görlitz was reached the compartment was nearly full. The other passengers were all tired-looking German civilians, seemingly inured to the long hours of slow traveling and to the constant demands for their papers. No word was said when the inevitable *SS* appeared, but the impression they gave was one of fear, as if they knew only too well that swift punishment would follow any objection. Leignitz came and went, and at long last, looking in utter weariness out of the window, Coward caught the name of Dresden and nudged Connolly awake.

They stretched and alighted, slinging their packs over their shoulders. Once again came the ordeal at the barrier, as their tickets and passes were scrutinized; then they had walked through and were out of the station.

"Blind old Pete," said Coward in relief, "I'll never grouse about the Enfield line tube again."

"They certainly make sure you have enough flippin' permits to travel," said Connolly. "Our passes will be worn out by the time we get to Lake Constance."

"Boy, oh boy. Just think, Wally—we're well on the way."

Strolling through the streets of Dresden, with a wary eye for soldiers and policemen, they looked for a quiet spot to rest in until the evening train left. A small park seemed best, and there they sat most of the day, munching chocolate and trying to forget how cold they felt. Being a pawn in this particularly grim game of chess was ceasing to be funny. The life of a hunted man is heavy with fear, and they were feeling the strain in no uncertain way.

Fifteen minutes before the train was due to leave at half past eight, they joined the queue at the booking office. Things went smoothly, the SS handed back the passes without comment, and once again they were jolting along toward their goal. Chemnitz was gained in the middle of the next morning and an air raid had evidently just finished. The station buzzed with noise as Germans emerged from the underground shelters they were compelled to take to at the first sound of a siren. Leaving the train, Coward and Connolly pushed through the crowds and booked to Ulm, the last town on their railway itinerary. Luckily the Ulm train left almost at once and, hardly able to believe their good fortune, the two settled down to endure the final lap.

Plumes of smoke were rising from the center of the city and one factory they passed blazed merrily, occasioning bitter remarks from the passengers. A big *Unteroffizier* of the *Wehrmacht* turned to Coward and snarled in hatred of the R.A.F. Connolly nodded, and Coward looked sympathetic. The *Unteroffizier* apparently found this lukewarm response unsatisfactory; to Coward's dismay he began to ask questions in a truculent tone. Connolly did his best to cope.

"We are Bulgarians," he chanted in his phrase-book

German. "We go to work at Ulm. These terrible raids, *ach,* it is cruel." He added *"Schweinehund* Churchill" for good measure, and closed his eyes hopefully. Somewhat mollified, the soldier followed suit, and Coward blessed the fact that he had this resourceful and fearless soldier from Liverpool as a comrade.

More towns, more *SS,* more checks, and still the luck held. Night came, passed without incident. Achingly hungry, both men resisted the temptation to eat some of their rations; the introduction of Cadbury's chocolate and Player's cigarettes into the life of that carriage was unthinkable.

Then, late the following night, the train steamed slowly into the platform at Ulm; they gathered their packs and prepared to alight. Everyone in the crowded station seemed to be wearing a uniform of some sort or another, making the two more conspicuous than ever.

"I don't like this, cocker," hissed Connolly.

"Don't hesitate now," replied Coward. "Keep on walking as if we come here every week."

"The dye on my trousers has run, damn it."

"Don't look at them. My clothes feel like a sack."

Threading through the motley assortment of service men, they hugged the side of the platform nearest the waiting rooms and offices until the barrier was near.

"Funny," said Connolly. "I never felt like this at the other places. Let's rest up for a minute."

"Wally, we can't. Suppose someone has noticed us already? If we show we're not sure of ourselves we're dead ducks. We've got this far, we can go the rest."

Tagging themselves behind a knot of people, they approached the barrier. Without a word, the senior of the *SS* men snatched their passes. He regarded the documents in silence, passed them to his companion, and stood looking at the prisoners with a faintly ironic light in his eyes.

Not daring to look away, Coward calculated wildly on the chances of running for it. Yet perhaps the *SS* were only playing with them; after all, the papers had survived all the other inspections since Kattowitz.

Receiving back the passes, the *SS* man looked at them again close. Raising his eyes, he smiled at Coward, a curiously twisted smile of enjoyment to come, and tapped the passes against his fingernails. Almost conversationally, in passable English, he inquired:

"But you are British, yes?"

7

RECAPTURE

Quick-witted Connolly rose to the occasion magnificently.

"British?" he repeated as if struggling to understand, and turning to stare questioningly at Coward. His face was pale. Suddenly the light appeared to dawn on him.

"British!" he exploded in his own brand of German. "No, no, no—we are Bulgarians, Bulgarians!"

"Ja, ja. Bulgarians," chipped in Coward desperately.

A little taken aback by the force of the rebuttal, the *SS* man stopped smiling. He glanced again at the documents in his hand.

"I think British," he said in English. "You come, please." He gestured them to follow him.

"No, no!" protested Connolly. "We are Bulgarians —we work in the mines."

The junior *SS* man prodded them to get moving; he walked behind them as they reluctantly made to follow the other. Connolly turned to appeal to him.

"We will miss our train," he almost shouted. "We are Bulgarians, Bulgarians!"

People were turning to look at them. The junior Nazi was perfectly impassive.

"Schweinehund Engländer!" exclaimed Coward, borrowing Connolly's earlier gambit and attempting to spit, but his mouth was too dry. He was filled with a crushing disappointment.

They entered a small office room a few yards away. There was a brief dialogue between the *SS* men and an elderly officer seated behind a trestle table. He took the documents and studied them for a minute.

"Where are you going?" he asked in English.

Connolly began to answer in German, realized his mistake, then plunged on as fast as he could, protesting that they were proceeding to take up work by Lake Constance. He was sweating visibly.

The German made no comment. Picking up a telephone at his elbow he gave a number, waited, then began to talk rapidly and loudly. Coward seized the opportunity to pass on a suggestion to Connolly in an undertone.

Replacing the receiver, the officer spoke again in English.

"So, you are Bulgarians, eh?"

Connolly shook his head in bewilderment. With a slight smile, the officer repeated the question in German.

"Yes," Connolly roared in reply, "and we demand to see the Bulgarian Consul!"

The officer chuckled; taking their cue, the SS men hooted with laughter, until with a glance he silenced them.

"Listen to me, you two," he said in his attractively lisping English. "The next time you have Bulgarian passports drawn make sure they are forged correctly." He held up the cards. "See, they are well done, very well indeed; you could say perfect except for one small thing. The eagle's head is pointing the wrong way." He smiled again. "Now then, who are you and what are you doing riding around Germany? Your passports were noticed at Chemnitz and we were telephoned to pick you up here." He waited for them to speak, then continued, "All right, let us not waste time. It is obvious you are British, it is obvious you are escaped prisoners, and it must be obvious to you that the longer you try my patience the harder it will go with you. Or, perhaps, if you stick to your fantastic story, you would prefer to be treated as spies?"

Abject in his misery, Coward shrugged.

"You win," he admitted. "We're British prisoners of

war all right, and you can get stuffed. Okay, Wal, you can light up your Player's now."

"I advise you not to be impertinent, my friend," said the German. "To escape and travel with forged documents is a serious matter; do not add to your trouble. I think you will be sorry before long that you ever embarked on this stupid adventure."

"All prisoners of war have the right to try to escape," returned Coward.

"Say 'Sir' when you address an officer. Prisoners may try to escape, however foolish that may be, but in disguising themselves as civilians and carrying forged identity papers, they make themselves liable to be shot as spies. Do you wear your uniforms under those clothes? No? Then you risk grave consequences. We are at war, not playing games."

Their packs were seized and emptied with relish by the *SS* men, their clothes searched and all food and incriminating material removed, and their personal details duly noted.

"What bloody awful luck," groaned Connolly, "after coming all this way."

"Never mind, boy," answered Coward. "The old dog is learning a few more tricks. They'll come in handy another time. Keep your eyes open—you never know."

A crumbling castle at Ulm was their billet for the next few days, and in the absolute blackness of one of its dungeons the two men lay on a damp stone floor and listened to an obscene scuffling around them. They had been brought by three guards from the local garrison after a severe beating in the station office room. For ten solid minutes an *Unteroffizier* and two privates had hammered them around the small room until their heads sang and blood spattered over their clothes. With yelps of pleasure mixed with curses, the Germans had expressed their hatred with such violence that it was all Coward and his companion could do to avoid hitting back, although well aware that the slightest retaliation would be met with a bullet. Eventually their bruised bodies had been kicked into a waiting van and the gates of the castle had closed behind them shortly afterward.

Two days passed in the total darkness, without a visitor of any kind. The continual rustling soon resolved itself into living walls of rats; each side of the dungeon was alive with movements as the creatures descended in a phalanx and crisscrossed the small space. Unable to sleep, the men took turns in pacing up and down, kicking their heels and making as much noise as possible to keep the rodents at reasonable length while the other tried to rest. Situated as they were without food or water, the ordeal would soon have come to an end in their deaths had not on the third day the door suddenly and unbelievably swung back and a guard appeared with cold coffee and a hunk of stale bread. They devoured the food like wolves, and it put new life in them. The guard this time left the grille of the iron door unlatched; they blinked drearily in the faint electric light that filtered through and managed rueful grins at their grimed and blood-bespattered appearance.

"Well, what happens now?" asked Coward.

"Oh, they're cooking up a nice surprise, you bet. Getting the honeymoon suite ready for us at the local Ritz, or digging our graves, maybe."

"I doubt that, thank God. If they'd meant to kill us, why give us food? Anyway, you dig your own grave in this lark. You're not sorry you came, are you, Wally?"

"Sorry? Wouldn't have missed this little turn-out for the world. Just think, I might have been wasting my time sunning my flippin' torso on a beach back home with nothing to do but feed my face and take a long cold beer, and in the evening if a nice popsie—"

He was interrupted by a second loud unbolting of the door. Two guards, rifles at the ready, motioned them out.

"Here goes," Coward murmured. "Hang on to your hat."

At the point of bayonets they were marched through the courtyard of the castle and out under the high postern gate. The medieval world was left behind them as they mounted a truck and jolted along the road back to the railway station. Under the eyes of a fresh brace of guards they waited for several hours at the end of a dank, cheerless platform, a necessary procedure to avoid corrupting the German population with the sight of Britishers, and at long last, so stiff they could barely move, boarded a train. A compartment had been reserved for them; they sat in silence on its hard wooden seats and watched the industrialized countryside flash past. Coward forgot his own troubles in wondering what had happened to Barney and Pilski, hoping they had managed to survive unhurt, and it was with a start that he heard one of the guards mention Stuttgart as the train drew into a large station. They clambered out and began a long walk through the streets, arriving at length at what had once been a block of stables but was now a filthy pile of buildings converted into a detention camp by the simple expedient of having it surrounded by barbed wire.

Thrust into a small, bare room, they were ordered to take off their civilian clothes, whose age had been increased considerably by the past few days, and dress themselves in two old uniforms of the German army that lay tossed on the floor. On Coward's jacket was the wilting eagle of the Third Reich, and this he was busy removing for decency's sake when a burly *Feldwebel* entered. The German stood for a second horrified at what he saw, then, enraged at the insult, he hit Coward into a corner with a resounding smack on the jaw and followed it up with two or three strenuous kicks to the ribs. Connolly made to intervene, but Coward waved him weakly back. The boot crashed into his groin, doubling him in agony. He struggled not to be sick as he dragged himself to his feet, pain coursing through his body. Connolly, growling with suppressed fury, helped him along to follow the *Feldwebel* out of the room.

"The dirty bastard," muttered the other. "If only I could have a go at him for two minutes."

"Don't worry," Coward gasped. "We'll get even."

They were led into a long room devoid of any furniture, beds, or covering on the concrete floor. It was filled to overflowing with prisoners. Men of a dozen nationalities crowded together on the floor, leaning against each other for some semblance of comfort and warmth; some of them gazed with a vague interest at the newcomers and tried to grin a welcome. With some difficulty, the two Britishers made a space for themselves and sat down. They were immediately questioned by those nearest, but pain and fatigue had done their work on Coward and he quickly passed into a deep coma from which not even the arrival of the evening meal, a raw turnip apiece, could arouse him.

As night drew on all the men attempted to lie down, fitting themselves into each other like a huge jigsaw of human forms. There were no latrines, so a corner of the room was utilized for the purpose of nature and this became so offensive that it was scarcely bearable, yet it had to be borne. If a man wished to turn, unable to suffer any longer in one position, all his neighbors had of necessity to turn with him.

At around midnight, when Coward had awoken from his sleep of exhaustion and was lying weak and ill on the floor, the door was flung open and a gruff voice called out:

"Der Englische Feldwebel?"

In surprise, he called back, "Yes?"

"Hier," said the voice.

Painfully he levered himself up and picked his way over the tightly packed forms to the door, unavoidably treading on hands and legs. Arriving at the door, he peered at the shadowy figure standing there. It was a weedy *Unteroffizier,* a man they had encountered on checking into the camp. The figure bent forward.

"Der Englische Feldwebel?" he repeated.

"Yes," said Coward again, suddenly filled with hope that orders for his removal might have come through.

The German spat full into his face; as he staggered in surprise the German moved back and slammed the door. Wiping the spittle from his cheek, Coward silently found his place again on the concrete.

"Who was it?" Connolly whispered.

"Some gent who didn't seem to like me. Gobbed right in my face. Don't ask me why."

Slowly he got back to a fitful sleep.

The next day passed without incident, except for the raw turnips, but when midnight came around Coward heard himself called to the door again. This time he was wary, but had to go for fear of the consequences if he ignored the order. Sure enough, another wad of spittle zoomed at his unprotected face in the darkness, followed by the slamming of the door. On the third night, tormented by the likelihood of a further summons, he was unable to sleep and lay awake in a misery of anticipation. When the call did come, he feigned sleep at first, then, hearing voices in the corridor, wondered if this might not be a genuine arrival of movement orders. He carefully remained out of range at the door, but was motioned by a guard into the corridor and along to a corner in it. Rounding it, he found himself confronted once more by the *Unteroffizier.*

"*Der Englische Feldwebel?*"

"Yes," said Coward, gritting his teeth.

It came; he wiped the phlegm from his eye and walked unsteadily back to the room, accompanied by howls of laughter. An attempt on the fourth night would probably have cost the German his life, whatever the consequences, but he must have sensed that the sport had gone far enough.

A few days later, while in conversation with a young Frenchman who had been recaptured after escaping from his working party, Coward learned that he had succeeded in smuggling into camp the set of passes he had used, and, incredibly enough, that they were absolutely genuine travel warrants to Stettin in the north. All Coward's native Cockney persuasion came into play and eventually the passes changed hands and were sewn neatly into the crotch of his trousers. Nothing, he thought cheerfully, could resist the wiles of a Londoner when he got into his stride with all the patter acquired from the stallholders of Petticoat Lane and the Caledonian Market. He donated his whole wealth, a sadly mangled cigarette, to the Frenchman in return.

At the end of about a fortnight, all the prisoners were ordered out into the stable yard and warned to be on their best behavior; an inspection was about to be made and woe betide any man who dared to complain to the visiting officers.

"This is our chance, Wally," Coward whispered. "If we stay here much longer we'll all pass out with hunger. I'm going to have a go."

From the gateway emerged two elderly German officers of fairly exalted rank. Coward started forward, only to be kicked back surreptitiously by the big *Feldwebel*, who had been eyeing him savagely. Cursing, he nursed his knee and waited for the officers to come abreast. As the first one approached, a stooping old fellow with a somewhat kindly face, Coward stepped smartly out of his rank and gave a parade ground salute. It used a good deal of his remaining strength, but evidently impressed the German, for he stopped and said in English:

"Yes? Who are you?"

"Sergeant-major Coward of the British Army, sir."

"What do you want?"

"I wish to complain of the unsoldierly treatment and brutality we have had from the guards here, sir, and of the lack of food and proper accommodation."

The officer looked startled and turned to speak rapidly to the *Feldwebel*, who blustered and stammered in reply.

"Come with me," said the officer to Coward. "I will hear your complaints."

With a meaning look at the smoldering *Feldwebel*, Coward followed the German to the office of the *Kommandant*, a worthy whom no one had seen or was to see. Standing strictly to attention, he recited his complaints one by one, stressing the inhumanity of the treatment of the prisoners and the animalistic conduct of the guards. The elder officer smiled slightly at the vigor of the story, then spoke sharply.

"Very well. I am satisfied that your complaints should be investigated and you have my word as a German officer that any wrongs will be put right. Furthermore, I will see that you are returned to your *Stalag* as soon as possible. I apologize for the behavior of the guards; in wartime we cannot always employ the best of men in the *Wehrmacht.*"

Knowing that he could rely on this old man, Coward expressed his thanks and saluted. The officer held up a detaining hand.

"One moment. I have spent many years of my life in London, Sergeant major Coward, and I can assure you that this war was not of my choosing. Naturally, perhaps, I hold that Germany is in the right but I would not wish that any of you British men should emerge from these bitter years thinking that all we Germans are bad enemies. Who knows, perhaps after it is all over you will be able to say you met some Germans who treated their prisoners in a humane manner and kept to the code of honorable warfare."

The result of this interview followed quickly. Within an hour the men were moved to a great harness room where clean straw lay on the floor and a latrine stood outside the door. And when hot soup and six hundred grammes of bread arrived for each man, Coward was acclaimed by all and sundry. British stock soared.

Some days later three guards appeared from Lamsdorf to escort the prodigals home. Again they gritted through the monotony and discomfort of the journey, although feeling some compassion for the guards who had tried to stay awake all the time. The Germans were considerably more tired than their prisoners when Lamsdorf camp was reached.

The first port of call was, as always, the search hut, and Coward feared for his hidden trove. But after stripping to the waist he convinced the searchers that his trousers were crawling with lice and so walked out with the precious load intact in the crotch. He drew an issue of British khaki from the Red Cross stores and wandered into the main body of the camp to meet his old friends again. They crowded around him and plied him with questions. There were several new faces, so he was guarded in his replies, waiting until he could speak privately to own comrades before passing on tips and encouragement.

At the weekend he was called to the administration office for trial. This was expected, of course, and he was prepared to spend several uncomfortable weeks in the cooler, though not without a struggle. He had, he felt, a card or two up his sleeve and mentally reviewed the prospects as he entered the adjutant's room and looked into the bucolic features of that excitable individual.

"So," grunted the adjutant pleasurably.

Coward waited, conscious that he was batting not only for himself but for his friend waiting in the anteroom. The adjutant barked a stream of German and the interpreter translated.

"The adjutant says you will suffer for having caused the German Government so much trouble and expense. He says that if you have nothing to say he will sentence you straight away."

Coward tut-tutted and the clicking of his tongue seemed to act on the adjutant like a goad on an ox. His face swelled.

"But I have something to say," Coward began, relaxing and leaning forward a little. "Private Connolly and I have been subjected to grossly inhuman treatment at the prison camp at Stuttgart. We have been kicked, punched, starved and spat at, contrary to the Geneva Conventions and in direct opposition to the terms of The Hague Treaty of 1926, of which Germany is a signatory."

Taken aback, the interpreter gaped at him. It was not usual for prisoners on trial to make any defense; as a rule they were only too content to accept their punish-

ment, generally two or three weeks in solitary confinement, and let it go. But this was not a usual prisoner:
Coward had rehearsed his lines for two days and had it
off pat. The little man translated the speech to the adjutant who burst into a roar like a bull and rose to
his feet, babbling in his anger until Coward cut him
short with an imperious gesture.

"Furthermore," continued the Britisher imperturb-
ably, "it stated distinctly in The Hague Treaty that all
prisoners of war shall have the right to escape if they
should wish to try to do so, and that when recaptured
the holding power should in no wise attempt to treat
them in an inhumane manner, meting out only sum-
mary justice, viz., a term of close imprisonment not
exceeding one month." He paused for breath while
the interpreter gabbled nervously to the adjutant.
"Now I intend as soon as possible to exercise my
rights as a British prisoner of war and inform the trus-
tees of the Convention of Geneva of my treatment and
that of my comrades at the hands of the Germans. I
shall ask for an immediate and full inquiry into the
circumstances surrounding the whole affair. Unless,
that is," he said, leaning farther forward until he spoke
into the adjutant's inflamed countenance, "unless you
undertake to dismiss the charge against Connolly and
myself."

As the interpreter conveyed this ultimatum, light
gradually dawned on the officer and this expression
became positively murderous. But caution was mixed
with anger and he must have known that Coward's
position was unassailable. Try as they would, they
could not stop a prisoner from eventually getting in
touch with Geneva, and the Germans were very shy
of any investigations into their treatment of Britishers.
They were afraid that reprisals might be carried out
against their own men in British hands and knew that
this would go down badly with the German people.
Slowly he drew himself up to his full height and in
German spoke at length and with great volubility to
Coward. He traced his ancestry from a she-goat to the

present representative of the family now standing smiling before him. He dwelt lovingly on the probable fate of that member and hoped fervently that he would suffer a thousand unpleasant deaths. At the end of his long discourse he hissed with outstretched arm, *"Gehen Sie!"*

"The *Herr Hauptmann* wishes you to go," stuttered the interpreter. "He says no charge will be made against you and that you and your friends will suffer no penalty. But he warns you never to cross his path again."

"Thank the gentleman for me," said Coward and walked out of the office. Connolly was waiting for him anxiously.

"What happened, Charlie?" he asked apprehensively.

"Happened? Nothing's happened, Wally. We're okay —no charge against us."

"No!"

"It's straight up. The adj. and I had a little comfy chat and made quite a nice bargain. I won't tell Geneva about Stuttgart and he won't interfere with our sleep."

"Well, if you're not a flaming beaut—"

Coward modestly agreed.

"You're a real gem, Charlie," enthused Connolly delightedly. "Wait till we tell the boys about this. But for Pete's sake, how did you do it?"

"I have my methods, Watson," Coward murmured. "Cigarette?"

A week later Coward was summoned to the office and handed a cable from Geneva. Apparently his wife back in England had not heard from him for several months and had written to the British War Office, who in turn had communicated with the authorities in Switzerland. The cable read:

"Welfare report requested on Sergeant-Major Coward."

A polite *Unteroffizier* passed him a blank form on which to compose his reply. He wrote:

Please to report am in fairly good health. Cause of

not writing through escapade. Treatment after recapture very good."

He returned the form to the soldier, who read it carefully.

"Thank you, Mr. Coward," he smiled.

"Don't mention it, cock," said Coward, and walked back to the peace of his barrack.

8

MURDER AT THE
SUGAR FACTORY

The dull monotony of life at Lamsdorf resumed its course. Jack Barney and Pilski, fortunately uninjured during their recapture, and their subsequent term in the cooler quickly a thing of the past, discussed with Coward and the irrepressible Liverpool man ways and means of making another attempt. Once again their names were entered on the list of volunteers for working parties and the shortage of competent men to take charge was so acute that Coward was assured his turn might come quite soon. In the event, however, several months were to drag past before he saw the outside of the camp again.

During his walks around the camp he stumbled one day upon a grisly fact. A constant stream of carts passed by one section of the wire and on investigation were found to be loaded with the dead bodies of Russians from a camp about half a mile away. A typhus epidemic was in full spate there; the daily toll of lives was unbelievably high, medical attention absolutely nil, and so the bodies of the many who succumbed were merely heaved on to the carts and trundled away to a great pit in the woods where burial took place without ceremony or the wasting of a moment's time.

The discovery incensed Coward and he straightaway set to work to find out more. There were, he guessed, almost a million Russians herded in the camp under conditions that made the spread of the disease certain; if something were not done, and done quickly, hardly one of the unfortunate wretches could hope to survive. In fact, shortly after he had first noticed the carts rolling by on their grim journey, the German authorities were forced to place the Russian camp in strict quarantine. The only motive in this belated act was to try to save the civilian population from infection; no sympathy or common humanitarianism was ever shown toward the Russians.

Determined to make an energetic protest to the German *Kommandant* of *Stalag VIIIB* about the method of burial, Coward was somewhat surprised to be received courteously. The tall, upright old man was a true German of the old school, and although hampered in his decency by the Teutonic brutishness of the adjutant, he did try to do his best for the men under his charge. He explained to Coward that he held no jurisdiction over the Russians but promised to protest himself at their crude burial and to attempt to have coffins made. He evidently succeeded, for a few days later the hearses in convoy were seen to be carrying neat wooden boxes stacked in piles. Coward felt he had achieved something at last: the Hun was at least open to a humanitarian appeal. His complacency and newfound trust was rudely shattered the very same evening when he watched the line of carts wending their way back from the woods, this time bearing a load of empty coffins. It was clear that the bodies had been shot out at the mass grave and the coffins retained for the next batch of dead.

The Russian camp was so near to Lamsdorf that it could be seen dimly on the far side of an enormous field. All the Russians were compelled to work, for the Soviet Union was not a member of the Red Cross organization or a signatory to The Hague Convention covering the treatment of prisoners of war. Officers and men alike shuffled out to the mines or forests, forced to work until they dropped, their rations at starvation level even for men having no work to do at all. A bullet quickly settled any sign of resistance.

The story was told to Coward of how, a year or so

back, an overflow of Russians were temporarily housed in a compound at Lamsdorf, remaining there for a month or so and becoming more fiercely hungry every day. One night, as they tried to cheer themselves by singing the plaintive laments of their native land, a German guard stopped outside a barrack hut to listen, holding his dog on a short lead. The songs' nostalgia completely lost on him, it presently occurred to his agile mind that it would introduce a spark of fun to set the dog on to them, making an anecdote that would surely earn an extra glass of beer the following evening in the *Gasthaus* in the village. So he slipped the lead off the brute and with a shout pushed it into the hut. Guard dogs were kept in a permanent state of savage hunger and required little inducement to attack any hapless individual found wandering the camp roads at night. This one went to work with a will; with a snarl it leaped inside and the guard listened with satisfaction to the cries and scuffling. After two or three minutes, however, the noises ceased. The dog did not reappear and the guard waited with increasing uneasiness in the heavy silence. He turned tail and walked off hurriedly. The next morning the skeleton of the beast was tossed out of the compound, picked clean. It had proved a welcome meal for the Russians, and the probability is that had the guard shown his face at the barrack door he would have undergone the same fate.

In spite of their suffering, the Russians were pleasant enough and seemed to be perpetually smiling. Chances to fraternize with them were rare indeed, yet a genuine camaraderie existed between them and the British, manifesting itself in a dozen different ways. From time to time the men of VIIIB held a whip-round for tins of food to be passed over to them, permission for this having been surprisingly granted; however ravenous their own appetites the British could always find something to contribute, if it were only a biscuit per man. In the heat of summer, when appetites were low, a great pile of tins awaited transport by cart to the camp across the fields.

At this time Wing Commander Bader of the R.A.F.* was brought to Lamsdorf; although an officer, he had made himself such a torment to the Germans at the R.A.F. Officers Camp of *Luft III* at Sargen, near Breslau, that he was sent to VIIIB as a punishment. Coward managed to have several conversations with him and learned much that he was able to use later on; indeed, one of Coward's closest friends was in due course to help to organize one of Bader's most sensational escapes, an attempt that was to ring around the world and hearten everyone serving the cause of freedom. The indomitable courage and fiercely uncompromising energy of the crippled hero who, without legs, continually rallied the prisoners to attempt new methods of escape, were not always popular in camp, but they brought out the best in everyone with whom he came into contact, and to Coward's spirits provided a badly-needed fillip.

With agonizing slowness the months of 1942 drew to a close, and with the year's end the news from the war fronts became more hopeful. Thoughts turned to Christmas and the theater began to resound with preparations for the grand Christmas pantomime. In November came word that the Red Cross in England were sending special parcels containing such luscious items as Christmas pudding, a tin of stewed beef and a tin of dehydrated eggs. This was good news indeed and the festive season was welcomed enthusiastically. As the time approached, each barrack sported paper chains contrived from the labels around the tins of food in Red Cross parcels and Coward's hut boasted a small twig of Christmas tree scrounged from a co-operative guard. The special parcels duly arrived and on Christmas Eve they were distributed; as a festive gesture the Germans forbore to puncture the tins, well knowing that the luxuries they contained would be scoffed without delay. With the ration issues of bread and potatoes

---

*See *Reach for the Sky*, the amazing story of Douglas Bader. Another volume in the Bantam War Book series.

increased for the occasion, the Britishers looked forward to a royal feast.

Coward sat in his hut with his pals, Digger and Connolly on one side and Dickie Spring of Liverpool on the other. They had heated their tins of beef and ate them with the potatoes, following up with plum pudding and hot tea. It was a good meal and left them uncomfortably full, for like all prisoners their stomachs were incapable of holding a meal of normal size.

That evening was a gala night in the theater, for it saw the first performance of the great panto, especially written for the occasion and entitled *Treasure Trove*. But as the converted hut held about three hundred men out of almost twelve thousand in camp, Coward and his friends were not successful in getting tickets. Instead they visited the barrack next door in the compound and saw a play performed on a small stage constructed by the simple expedient of pushing six tables together and covering them with a couple of blankets. The play was Shaw's *Arms and the Man* and the Chocolate Soldier in it was a young airman who had newly arrived at Lamsdorf, a sergeant pilot named Denholm Elliot. His acting was superb, even in that confined space and with a heroine who labored under the handicap of a baritone voice and revealed muscular arms beneath her "dress." It was the perfect end to a fine evening; they went to their bunks and snuggled under their blankets, shouting Christmas greetings to each other down the length to the hut, confident and happy in their comradeship. For an hour or so it had been good to be alive.

Christmas morning revealed a fall of several inches of snow and still more floated thickly down as they were roused from their beds and prodded out on to the parade ground by the bayonets of the guards. Huddled in their greatcoats they waited while the counting game began, longing for the end of the farce so they could scamper back to the warmth of the bunks. But it was not to be. The Australians and South Africans whooped with joy at seeing snow for the first time and very soon a great snowball battle had developed.

It was at this moment that the adjutant was descried approaching along the road, together with the *Kommandant* and two guards, all laughing heartily at the battle and clearly taking it as an illustration of the feeble intellects of the prisoners. As they drew near the exchange of snowballs suddenly stopped dead and the *Kommandant,* who knew his British well, stopped and spoke to the adjutant. The latter shook his head in obvious disagreement and made as if to walk on, only to be stopped again as the *Kommandant* remonstrated with him. The fellows watched breathlessly. It was apparent that the *Kommandant* was saying, "I shouldn't go past them, if I were you, *Herr Hauptmann.* They'll chuck snowballs at you," and his junior was equally obviously replying in indignation, "They wouldn't dare!" Then the *Kommandant* was seen to shrug his shoulders and the two men continued slowly forward, the elder raising his collar in wary anticipation of the onslaught. As they entered the road dividing the two compounds a voice rose loud and clear in the frosty air.

"Let the bastards have it, boys!"

A perfect barrage of snowballs descended on the wilting officers and their hapless bodyguards. Forced to run the gauntlet until they were out of range, the adjutant's face was empurpled with fury and the *Kommandant's* shaking with suppressed mirth. He waved a hand to the lads, now cheering triumphantly, and drew the adjutant away, leaving the battlefield to resume its previous disposition. Barrack discussion that evening was decidedly pro-*Kommandant.* He was quite a decent old stick, it was agreed; almost a pity, really, that he was German. The men realized that had he not been present they would have fared very differently from the hands of the adjutant; he was a nasty bird to cross at any time, and would probably have used his revolver with some effect.

By New Year's Day the snow was so thick that walking in it had become difficult, but Coward, summoned

to the office of the *Arbeitsführer,* had no alternative but
to wade through it. Barney had just returned to Lamsdorf from a working party and the call had interrupted
a pleasant chat over a cup of tea. The *Arbeitsführer* was
the lieutenant in charge of working parties and Coward
wondered whether at last his turn had arrived again.
Reaching the office, he rapped on the inner door and
entered, finding the officer peering up at him from behind the usual trestle table.

"Ah, Mr. Coward. Yes . . . Mr. Coward." The
German looked reflectively at the Britisher and allowed
a slight smile to cross his pale face. Coward suspected
that he was in for a rough time.

"Did you want me?" he asked.

"Tell me, don't you salute an officer in your army?"

"Of course."

"Then salute me before you speak!"

Coward started dramatically and looked closely at
the shoulders of the lieutenant.

"Sorry, sir, but I don't know German ranks very
well. Never sure of the difference between the pips of
an officer and a *Feldwebel.*" He executed a shaky salute which would have turned his previous charges on
English parade grounds white with horror. The German
was not in the least put out and continued in silky
tones.

"There is a considerable difference between the
pips—did you call them?—and I advise you strongly
to learn it. Now let us proceed to another matter." He
lit a cigarette and carefully exhaled the smoke into
Coward's face. "I believe that the last time you went
out on a working party, you tried to escape. Am I correct?"

"There was a little misunderstanding, yes."

"Ah, a little misunderstanding," repeated the German slowly.

"But the adjutant put it right and we see quite eye
to eye on the matter."

"So. That must be nice for you." The German regarded Coward for some seconds before he spoke

again. "Let me give you two further points of advice," he said quietly. "First, to correct these 'misunderstandings' of yours with all speed. Second, not to attempt impertinence with me, or you will be very sorry, my friend."

"If you care to ask the adjutant—"

"Be silent. I am speaking. We do not hold your ridiculous escape against you, Coward. On the contrary, we know it is your duty to try to get away, the same as you are aware of our duty to shoot you if we catch you at it. Don't interrupt. We want you to take charge of another working party, this time at a sugar factory. You will leave tomorrow. That is good, yes?"

Coward was suspicious, but he answered, "Right. I'm ready any time."

The officer smiled again, playing contentedly with a paperknife.

"Good. You will move immediately to the *arbeits* compound and be ready to leave in the morning. Take some supplies from the Red Cross; your men out there are expecting you and you will want some medicines and things."

Convinced that there was something wrong somewhere, Coward saluted perfunctorily and withdrew. Back in the barracks he confided his misgivings to Digger and Barney.

"Wait a minute," said the South African. "Haven't I heard some queer stories about a sugar factory—beatings, or something?"

"Well, that'll be nothing new," answered Coward grimly.

"No, I don't mean by the Jerries."

"What are you talking about?"

"I may be wrong, but I seem to have heard something about the boys at one sugar factory being a bit round the bend."

"We're all round the bend, aren't we?"

"There've been some nasty scraps there, I believe."

"Where is this place? Do you know?"

"In Czechoslovakia somewhere, I think."

"Crikey, I hope not. Who's been in charge?"

"No idea. Look Charlie," Barney was suddenly very serious. "Are you going to make a break?"

"What the hell d'you think I'm going for—winter sports?"

"Well, for Christ's sake watch your step. Seems to me the Jerries might be cooking something up for you."

"Hope they are," said Coward lightly. "Could do with a couple of bangers and onions." But he shared Barney's doubt and lay awake that night trying to make sense of the Germans' unexpected new trust in him.

His examination in the search hut next morning was thorough, but not so thorough as to include unsealing the box of Red Cross medical supplies beneath which were secreted the passes obtained from the French boy at Stuttgart. Two guards accompanied him to the station and, after a freezingly cold wait, on to a train. The journey was slow, seeming even more interminable than usual, and Coward was practically past caring when one of the guards mentioned that they had crossed the border into Czechoslovakia and, later, that they were nearing a place called Stadt-Bau and must prepare to get off. Coward tried to fix in his mind the position of the station in the small town, but the intense cold numbed his efforts at reasoning and calculation; plodding through the snow, he was filled with depression at what might lie ahead. Yet at the sugar factory gates he was met by a stubby *Unteroffizier* of doubtful aspect who surprisingly wrung him by the hand and made him welcome.

"Why the red carpet?" Coward asked suspiciously.

The man's English was poor, but his actions were unmistakable. In a mixture of hand-waving, smiles, and broken phrases, he summed up that eternal proposition that has been echoed down the years by so many N.C.O.s of all services: if Coward played ball with him, he would play ball with Coward.

"The sergeant major last one was a very good man," he grated. "He made men work very hard. I make sergeant major nice billet. We friends too, eh?"

This did not sound good at all. Coward thought he had better tread warily.

"I hope so," he said. "Well, where are the men? I'd like to talk to them and get bedded down."

The *Unteroffizier* led the way to a high building and puffed up a flight of stairs, showing him into his bedroom, a small space separated by a wall from that of the German duty N.C.O.

"Where do the men sleep?" asked Coward, dumbfounded at having a room to himself.

"Zey sleep onder here," answered the German. "Zey are lazy—need *gut* sergeant major work zem."

"Oh, do they? Well, let me see them and have a chat. Perhaps we can come to an arrangement."

The *Underoffizier* beamed. "*Gut, gut.* Go down. You find zem all right."

Coward nodded and made his way downstairs. On the ground floor the entrance to the barrack was marked in large letters: *Shut the——door*. He went in. Along one side of the large room stood the usual rows of wooden bunks; facing them, and looking at him stood thirty or so men. In amazement he noticed that several of them held pieces of iron or logs of wood. On his immediate right a small dark man stepped forward, opening in his hand a cutthroat razor. Coward spoke quickly and with a bluff heartiness.

"Hullo, blokes. Nice sort of welcome this is, I must say. Who the hell d'you think I am, bloody Hitler? What are all the tools for?"

Nobody answered.

"Well don't look so bloody happy, the lot of you."

Still nobody spoke. In the cold eyes fixed on him he read a piercing, consuming hatred, the eyes of his fellow men filled with the desire to hurt, perhaps to kill. He looked around at them and felt the sudden constriction of fear in his throat.

"Come on, lads," said Coward after a pause. "What's all this about? My name's Coward; let's get acquainted and then you can tell me what's wrong." He turned to the man with the razor. "And put the chivvy away, Bill, unless you're going to have to shave. What's the idea, anyway?"

"It's to do you with," replied the man, with quiet venom. There was a murmur from his mates.

"All right," Coward said, "do me then. But just give me the reasons why. You're not the bloody Gestapo, you know—Britishers usually tell a man what he's guilty of before they beat him up. And I thought only Eyeties used knives for the job."

A burly Aussie, his battered hat jammed on his head, took a step forward.

"Look, mate," he said, "that kind of crap won't go down with us. We know you've come here to shake us up and increase the production of the factory, like the last bastard did. I reckon he's going to spend quite a time in the Lazarette and we decided that this time we'd show you which way the wind's blowing right from the start. That's how we feel, jacko, and you can please yourself which way you have it."

Coward knew the crisis was over; he laughed.

"Oh, come off it. Do I look like a perishing Jerry? So the last bloke ended up in the hospital. What did he do?"

"Tried to work the hell out of us, that's what. Lived like a lord himself—got everything he wanted from the fat slug of an *Unteroffizier* in exchange for working us like niggers on the sugar."

"You can't be made to do more than a fair day's work. Didn't you protest to the Jerry officers?"

"Too right we did. They sent in a squad of *SS* and beat the living daylights out of us with their natty little coshes."

"So you laid into the sergeant major."

"We settled him fine—you wouldn't have recognized him when they took him away. Then the Jerries tell us there's another man coming who's got their bleedin' interests at heart and he'll soon show us a thing or two. So if that's the way you aim to have it, they can take you away on your back too, and double quick."

"Now, listen to me. I can see now I was tricked into this working party because the Germans hoped you'd do just that. There hasn't been much love lost between us lately. I go on a working party for only two reasons: to cause as much damage as I can, and to escape."

"How do we know that?" snapped the man with the razor.

"You don't. You can only wait and see what happens. For a start, how many here want to escape?"

There was a chorus of assent.

"Right. Leave it to me. From my bedroom up there I'll have a good chance to keep an eye out for you. We'll organize a break for the earliest moment. What d'you say?"

So it was settled; Coward retired to bed that night, savoring to the full the delight of his new privacy, and wondered if he had really won the confidence of the men. But it was to prove quite a lengthy process to break down the legacy left by the former sergeant major.

Sabotage helped: while assiduously applying himself to the tasks of adapting copies from his own maps and hiding away any odd tin of rations which could possibly be spared, he guided the men in the several little acts of sabotage they could practice, and mysterious things happened to the consignment of sugar leaving the factory each day. It was soon discovered, for instance, that a fire started in a small cardboard box which was then thrust hurriedly into the center of a load of loose sugar would smoulder for hours before bursting into life in the open air and igniting the whole load. The sugar was poured in four-ton lots into specially built railway wagons, saving the cost of packets, and the trucks were ideal for fire tactics, spontaneous combustion not being unknown for their particular freight. Other peculiar things happened to the factory machinery and although this activity was kept to a minimum to avoid unnecessary suspicion, it helped Coward to establish his own integrity in the prisoners' eyes.

Their trust was finally captured, however, by the affair of the *Unteroffizier*.

This unattractive individual had lost no time in making himself the bane of Coward's life, besides being a constant menace to the well-being of the men. His habit of brandishing his revolver in the air when excited had once resulted in a bullet in the leg for a British soldier ordered to work faster, and everyone was therefore especially wary of angering him. He would come into the barracks when the men were having a meal and help himself to several cups of Red Cross coffee, a boon to a German deprived of the real substance for so many years. There were mutterings about his arrogance, and after he had enjoyed liberal portions of Coward's tea or coffee for a number of times running, it was as much as the other could do to restrain himself from pitching the swine through the window; but any such action could only end in disaster. The situation was not long, though, in coming to a head.

Busily engaged one evening in carefully tracing maps in his bedroom, Coward was interrupted by a blond Geordie whose job it was to keep a look-out on the stairs during the progress of the work.

"What's up, Harry? Goons?"

"No—everything's dead quiet."

"What is it, then? Something biting you?"

"That blasted Kussel the *Unteroffizier,* that's what's biting me."

"Blimey, has he turned cannibal now?"

"You can laugh, Charlie, but it's happened to a lot of the boys. Y'see, we wanted some *schnapps* from the town and that perishing Jerry said he'd get it for us if we gave him the money. We let him have all the *Lagergeld* we had, a damn sight more than the stuff is worth, and the dirty swine has just hung on to it. He says if we try to do anything about it he'll report us to the Gestapo and get them to do us over."

"He will, eh? Why the blazes didn't you come to me to get the stuff for you?" Slight though the men's complaint was, Coward knew that it was just the kind of further irritation that might drive them to desperation; the dearest immediate wish of some of the prisoners was for a night's drinking.

"Some of the chaps have asked me to have a word with you about it, Charlie. Can you do something?"

"Could have done a darned sight more if you'd trusted me in the first place."

"But can't we teach the little slob a lesson—"

"Lessons are no good for anyone like him. His hide's too thick and in any case you'd get a bloody quick reprisal."

"So we've just got to let him get away with it!"

"I didn't say that. Let's see, only yesterday he knocked out two of Fleming's teeth for slacking— quite a handy bloke with that revolver of his, isn't he? I was going to store that little incident up until the next visiting officer did his rounds, but it seems as though we'll have to deal with Mr. Kussel now."

Geordie grinned. "I knew you'd think of some way. How are you going to do it?"

"You'll see. It would certainly be helpful to have him out of the way for our break. My conscience will rest easy after all if I can settle a score or two with that devil."

Coward got up from the bed and walked over to the Red Cross box containing first aid kit and sedatives.

"Let's go downstairs, Harry, and have a cup of coffee. Tell all the boys to make some and for Christ's sake to leave my mug alone. Go on, look lively."

In a minute or two he heard from below the sounds of stoking up the small copper used for boiling water for drinks. From the Red Cross box he took an empty bottle and into it he poured as many different drugs as he could find: some twenty M & B tablets, crushed, three phials of morphia, and the entire remaining stock of cocaine. He gave the concoction a vigorous shake, inspected it with satisfaction, then corked the bottle and slipped it into his pocket. When he reached the *Wachstube* below, the water was just coming to the boil.

"Coffee ready, blokes?" he called out.

"What about tea for a change?" demanded the "brew-king," loudly. "We had coffee this morning."

"I know we did, old chum, but coffee is what our pal Kussel likes and coffee is what he's going to get. It's brass-monkey weather outside and with a bit of luck he'll be in as usual to drink some of it for us."

The "brew-king" stared at him open-mouthed; then he grinned.

"Okay, skip, just as you say. Coffee it is."

As soon as the coffee was ready, it was dished out into the men's mugs by the "brew-king." Coward sat by the door with Harry and Thompson the Australian; he dispensed the contents of the bottle into half a mug of coffee and stirred an abundance of sugar from the communal store filched from the factory. The other two watched him in incredulous silence and started violently when in due course the door opened and in came a beaming Kussel, his ratlike face aglow with anticipation. In his hand he bore an enormous and brand new mug, which he set down on the table with a crash.

"See, I bring my own mug, *ja?* One litre holds, is *gut*. I like coffee not half, eh?"

"All right, guts-ache," said Coward with a grimace. "Go on, help yourself."

Kussel needed no second invitation. He grunted with pleasure and emptied all three of the steaming cans into his own, then sat down and sniffed at the coffee appreciatively.

"*Gut, gut,*" he pronounced and drank the lot down in a mighty draught that left him gasping.

"Pretty good, eh?" asked Coward, rising.

"Ver' *gut*. Why you go? Sit down, talk."

"No, no, it's late, *Unteroffizier*. Time you were in bed, you know."

"*Nein, nein*. Is not late." The German's head drooped a little. "Mus' talk."

"Look, you're tired. Best get along before the snow gets too thick outside."

"Ach, jawohl." Kussel laughed, somewhat foolishly, and heaved himself to his feet. *"Gute Nacht,"* he mumbled. *"Gute Nacht,"* he repeated, turning and staggering out into the night.

"Christ, he's as pie-eyed as an owl," exclaimed Harry.

Thompson chuckled. "Don't know what you laced that coffee with, Charlie, but it looks as if you've given him a free drunk."

"I'm not so sure," said Coward thoughtfully.

The next morning a strange *Unteroffizier* appeared, a mild-looking man with gold-rimmed spectacles.

"Has *Unteroffizier* Kussel gone on leave?" Coward asked.

The man clucked like a frightened hen.

"Terrible. He was found dead in the snow last night, just outside the factory. Must have been his heart."

Coward sighed. "Well, who'd have thought it? Looked healthy enough to me, though he did like to drink."

"Ah, so? Poor man, poor man."

"Yes, we'll certainly all miss him."

Later when work for the day was over, Thompson came up to Coward's room and held out his hand.

"You're okay, Charlie," he said quietly. "That was a beautiful job you did on Kussel, and took a hell of a lot of guts, too."

"Don't speak too soon, Tommy. I'm sweating on the inquest now."

"Well, don't. There won't be one."

"Won't be one?"

"No. One of the lads has heard that the local garrison quack has certified natural causes."

"But that's—"

"I know it's crazy, but maybe the Jerries don't bother too much about a dead Kussel—I know I wouldn't! Anyway, apparently they're satisfied. Old Kussel had a reputation for hotting up his guard duties, you know. They just think he went out like a light."

"Stone the crows, that calls for a celebration."

"Hold it a minute. It calls for something else, too. When you came here you told us you'd help us make a break."

"Of course I will. The maps and stuff are nearly ready. But we've got to work out a scheme very carefully."

"There's no need to do that."

"No need? What d'you mean?"

"We had the idea long before you came and worked it all out, but we weren't ready. Guess we didn't really trust you until now, but old Kussel has changed all that. We'd like to have you in on it."

"Well, I'm damned! How are you going?"

"Through the washroom ceiling. It's taken months to chip a slab loose in the roof."

"And you managed to keep it dark even from me!"

"Half the boys are commandos, you know. Had plenty of training in that kind of thing."

"But every night your coats and trousers are locked away before lights-out."

"The door to the locker room has been fixed for weeks: we can open it whenever we want. But you'd help us a lot if you kept watch from your room over the washplace."

"You bet your socks I will! Have any of you made a break before?"

"No, I don't think so."

"Well, there's a tip or two I can pass on. Get the men together tonight and I'll talk to them. How many are going?"

"Fourteen or fifteen."

"H'm, quite a party. Fixed a date yet?"

"Sometime soon, but perhaps you can advise us."

In the barracks that night Coward inspected the extraordinary assortment of civilian clothes and adapted battledress that the men had managed to secrete away; he handed out the maps and passes so far completed and addressed them on important do's and don't's. He undertook to work out a timetable of the guards' movements and satisfied himself on the pairing arrangement which the men were to adopt once they were clear of the wire. He would, he hoped, see them off safely, then make a break himself a week later, although that might be especially difficult after the Germans had been alerted. With the mounting excitement around him, he was completely happy. Once again life had purpose and hope.

The documents took three weeks to complete and, as luck would have it, the night selected obligingly took on a useful mist. Coward said goodnight to the *Obergefreiter* occupying the room above his, and turned in early to snatch two or three hours' sleep. At midnight he rose and dressed; watch in hand, he stood at his window, peering out into the night and counting off the minutes. The timetable had taken many sleepless nights to compile and he prayed that it would hold good. The tension of that mass escape from Stadt-Bau has already been mentioned; it seemed that dawn could not be far away before the hands on his watch crept to one o'clock and he knocked on the floor to the men below, heard the creak of concrete slab as it lifted from the outhouse roof, and watched the figures scuttle away toward the wire. The awful period of waiting until the guard next came around, then, with an immense relief, he knew they had made it.

A good show, he thought as he undressed and climbed back into bed; now for his turn. His turn! He sat suddenly bolt upright. Of course; why not go now? After all, he had all his plans made. He had the papers that would pass him through to Stettin; he had money and a complete suit of clothes. Why wait until the whole countryside was roused? He could go now, through the hole in the wire made by others, and be saved all the explanations to the Germans in the morning when the *Appell* revealed fifteen bodies short. Hurriedly he dressed, adjusting the unfamiliar clothes, retrieved from under a floorboard, with cold hands. He had managed to acquire a collar and a lurid tie that made him look like a promising spiv; together with a black overcoat he really looked the part of a rather speedy civilian.

"Here goes," he muttered and lowered himself from the window on to the roof of the outhouse. Thank God they had closed the slab after them! Throwing his rucksack down on the ground first, he followed suit and immediately fell flat. The guard was passing again; Coward watched him anxiously as he came up to the hole in the wire, stopped, bent to look closer, then straightened in alarm and fired two blasting rifle shots into the air. The reports were deafening; their echoes had scarcely died away before the German began to scramble back to the guardhouse, bellowing *"Raus! Raus!"*

Trembling Coward leaped to his feet and dashed to the wire. Wriggling frantically through the gap, he could hear souts and whistles. His clothes caught on the barbs and he wrenched at them in desperation. At last he was free on the other side and running like a man possessed. Once he pitched headlong into a drift of deep snow and lay there for a time panting and summoning his strength. A dreaded noise spurred him into sudden action—the barking of dogs. Up again and on, ripping himself on thorns and receiving blow after blow from the branches that impeded his almost blind progress.

Eventually, after how long he could not tell, he came to an open space and in front of him lay salvation. A railway line cut across the forest and before his grateful eyes a goods train stood waiting under a signal. Making for the middle of the train, he strained for the sight of the guard; but the escaping steam from the engine seemed to be the only movement. At the first open car he reached up and swung himself aboard, using every ounce of will power to scale the high sides. Whatever he fell on was soft; bitterly cold, but comfortingly soft. He burrowed down and spread his coat like a blanket over himself.

An oblivion of exhaustion claimed him just as the wagon jolted into motion; wherever he was going he had not the remotest idea, but that he was indeed going was certain.

9

ALONE

The night was cruelly long and cold. Coward awoke to find his coat covered with a light fall of snow; the contact of his body had produced a puddle of icy water beneath him. Half frozen, he moved his arms and sat up. The dark shapes of trees moved past against a heavy sky, like an interminable procession of bent old men. He was on the run again: the thought snapped him into alertness.

With numbed fingers Coward opened his rucksack and munched one or two biscuits, telling himself he felt warmer by doing so. He conjured pictures of home and of his arrival there, of the delight of his family and friends, and the wonderful luxuries of warm feet and a good meal. He thought of the other escapers and how they were faring, of Lamsdorf and the adjutant, of Scouse and Digger and Barney and what they were up to. Almost desperately, he set his mind to work on painting mental canvases, occupying the grim and weary hours as they dragged on their course.

Dawn, when at long last its first streaks did appear, found him haggard and agonisingly stiff. From the direction of the rising sun he could see he was traveling due south, directly away from his objective of Stettin. He peered at his map and guessed that the train might be heading for Bratislava, and began to rationalize his position. One might be able to jump a train from there to Vienna; come to think of it, that might turn out a very good thing: it was always a good plan to travel away from one's objective at first and so confuse any pursuers. From Vienna there was a railway to Prague, and then, by way of Dresden, to Stettin. A long trip, it was true, but perhaps his food would hold out if he strictly rationed himself. To attempt to buy meals at station buffets was much too dangerous; his German was poor and would certainly collapse under serious questioning, and though his papers gave his identity as French, his knowledge of that tongue was limited to a few impolite phrases.

The train was traveling at a fast speed for a goods and he surmised that it was probably a special delivery of materiel for one of the warfronts. The sky began to clear, a relaxing warmth sank into his bones from the strengthening sun, and, almost suddenly, he felt an enjoyment in his strange journey. They were now passing through quite a mountainous district—the Carpathians, he judged—and the sheer beauty of the landscape was breathtaking after his last two years of gloom and crudity in prison camp surroundings. Sheathed in glittering snow, towering peaks encompassed the train on either side; once he saw a castle clinging to a hillside like one of the colored plates in the books of his childhood. Then the mountains gradually fell away and the train entered a dense forest. In its many clearings, he could see wood mills in full swing and smoke billowing from small factories which had mushroomed under the impact of war. He looked over the side of the wagon toward a smudge of smoke on the horizon, hoping it might mean they were nearing Bratislava, then stiffened as his eyes caught a large sign at the side of the track. *No stopping,* he translated, *German Government Experimental Station.*

Intrigued, he watched particularly closely, and presently passed two extensive factory buildings with a large loading ramp on to the track and neatly stacked rows of huge cylinders. A moment later the train had entered a tunnel and, warning sign notwithstanding, was grinding to a halt with clanking buffers and creak of brakes. On an impulse, he struggled into his coat, snatched up his rucksack, and swung himself over the side. He waited, flattening himself against the wall of the tunnel until the train shuddered into motion again;

when it had gone, leaving the air thick with smoke, he trudged back along the sleepers and cautiously re-emerged into the winter sunshine.

There was nobody to be seen. He walked boldly up to the ramp and inspected the nearest row of cylinders. They were even more enormous close up, looking vaguely like an airplane without wings or tail, but with a large cap screwed into the nose. Perhaps they were colossal shells, Coward mused, then dismissed the thought. Bombs were much more likely, and gas bombs likelier still. He made a mental note of their dimensions and design, recording, before returning to the track, the mark painted on their obscenely bulging bellies: V1.

The town was not very far, not more than two or three miles through the tunnel and along the track, though he walked farther, having to take to the fields as the suburbs appeared. Before long, he was treading the roads of Bratislava. The utter misery of the people he passed in the streets had to be seen to be believed. Hunger stared from their eyes, and by comparison with theirs, Coward's clothes, damp and unkempt as they were, looked positively smart. Crushed and beaten, these wretched Czechs existed only to serve their German overlords.

By trial and error, for he dared not ask the way, Coward found the railway station and came upon a sight which was to be only too familiar later on but now filled him with shock and futile anger. Across the square shuffled a column of Jews, apparently marching away to work. There were about two thousand of the poor creatures, led along like cattle by a dozen or so German soldiers. Filthy, wrapped in sacking and torn rags, their feet bare to the rough cobbles, blue with cold in the snow, they stumbled on their way unseeingly. All humanity seemed to have been squeezed from them; they were reduced to brute beasts. Sickened, Coward turned away from the spectacle, realizing that it was impossible to even tell their sex; men and women were indistinguishable. Coward was not a pious man, but this first encounter with Hitler's

Aryan racial policy brought a prayer to his lips for the
beings he had just seen, and burning hate in his heart
for men who could inflict such horror on their fellow
humans.

But the immediate problem was to get a ticket.
Trying to appear nonchalant, feeling horribly conspicuous, he forced himself to enter the station booking
hall and looked down a timetable board. There was a
train to Vienna in a few minutes. He pulled out his
money and stepped firmly up to the booking office window.

"*Wien, bitte,*" he said with a dry throat.

The girl inside the glass cage smiled at him; she was
a Czech and shared the friendly disposition of her people toward most foreigners.

"*Arbeitskarte?*" she asked.

A workman's ticket, Coward thought quickly.

"*Ja,*" he answered.

His fingers closed greedily on the ticket and he
hurried away, with foreboding, to the *SS* man at the
barrier.

"*Frankreich, ja?*" grunted the German.

He agreed, seized back the pass, and followed the
signs to his platform. The train arrived punctually and
he chose an empty third-class compartment, wondering in his relief how many more times he would have
to face that ordeal. The journey to Vienna was un-
eventful, his pass being demanded only once at the
Austrian border, and as it was genuine he presented it
with comparative confidence. It was seven in the
evening when the train reached the dim vault of the
main station of Vienna, and surviving the almost per-
functory inspection at the barrier he felt quite elated
and cocksure. The buoyancy soon vanished when he
had sought out a timetable. Apparently the trains for
Prague were few and far between: the next was at 2
p.m. the following day, a wait of nineteen hours. About
him milled crowds of people, mostly in service dress,
intent on catching their trains. Pulling himself together,
he put up his coat collar and wandered out into the
street. Snow was falling fairly heavily; it was obviously

out of the question to spend the night in the open air, yet to remain in the station all that time might well attract the interest of the police.

He walked aimlessly for an hour or more. All the stories he had heard of this gay city came tormentingly to his mind, but they were far from the truth now. The Vienna of wartime was shabby and depressing; fine buildings were dirty and lifeless. German uniforms were everywhere, and the night clubs and beer gardens had long since been converted into administrative offices for the *Wehrmacht*. Coward passed dimly lighted shops and looked longingly in at the cafés. Nothing in the world seemed more desirable than a hot drink, yet the risk was so great that prudence held him back. But eventually his resolution wavered, and he walked through the freezing snow until he found a suitably nondescript shop in a back street, paused while he wrestled again with the decision, then entered it, making, in his desire to appear at ease, almost unnecessary noise.

There were few people inside and he was able without difficulty to take a table in a corner from which he could watch the door. Behind a counter a fat woman sat reading a newspaper; for some reason Coward dreaded her looking up at him, but she was far too engrossed.

He settled himself and stole a cautious look around. The back of his chair practically touched that of a woman; she was leisurely paring her fingernails, her head completely hidden from his view by the hood of her coat. He raised his eyes and suddenly met those of a man in a raincoat, a man with an incredibly lean and fleshless face who was steadily regarding him from the opposite side of the room. For a moment Coward stared back, transfixed, while his blood raced; his mind instantly assessed the possibility of a dash to the door.

A sneeze at his side made him start violently. The waitress apologized and asked for his order.

"Er—*Kaffee, bitte*," he mumbled, aware that his confusion had been closely observed. God, he thought,

I must get out of this quickly. But if I run for it, the game will be up with a vengeance, and with a pack of them on my heels I'll never last five minutes outside.

The *ersatz* coffee arrived and he sipped the revolting liquid gratefully, feeling its warmth steal into him and seeming to penetrate his very bones.

Take it slowly, he told himself; if that is the *Gestapo* over there, he isn't sure of himself. Ignore him; fix your mind on something else. Think of the kids at home, or those cylinders by the railway, or the Jews being marched to work. He's still looking. Never mind, relax, act naturally. What are you going to do if you rush out, anyway? If he's an agent, he'll follow you and soon discover you've nowhere to go. You've got a few minutes to think of something fast; use them. You can go back to the station and lock yourself in a lavatory, pretending you're sick, or try to catch a bus out of town for a while——

"*Guten Abend.*"

He turned in surprise and looked into the face of the woman. Heavily caked powder could not conceal the deep lines of age and dissipation, and thin hard lips were clearly visible below the grotesque crescents of thick scarlet paint. He repressed a shudder and murmured:

"*Guten Abend. Nicht verstehe der Deutsche.*"

She looked vaguely interested. "So? *Warum nicht?*"

"Er—*Ich Frankreich.*"

She nodded, twisted her mouth into a smile that her cold eyes belied, and looked him up and down in a manner no doubt intended to be coquettish. A gust of her cheap perfume carried with it a momentary image of the back alleys of Piccadilly, and suddenly Coward knew he had the answer. Here was undoubtedly a woman of the streets; it would make a big drain on his money, but if he went with her he would have an ideal resting place for the night, with warmth and sleep. They were all the same; she would probably think him soft in the head, but if he paid in advance and made it clear that he was interested only in a bed and sleep, she would almost certainly just shrug it off and count it a night's easy money. Yes, it was the answer. Controlling his stomach's revulsion, he summoned a smile back.

She put away her nail file with an affected daintiness and whispered, *"Kommen Sie mit?"*

"Ja," he breathed. *"Wieviel?"*

Opening her eyes wide, she murmured back, *"Das ist mir ganz egal."*

So she didn't care how much, eh? Of course, custom would be bad on a night like this. He finished the dregs of his coffee, meeting over the rim of the cup the unwinking stare from across the room. It was now or never.

"Komm," he said, rising. He paid his bill, shrinking from the contempt in the glance of the fat woman who received his money, and followed his companion out of the door, expecting at every step to feel a restraining hand on his shoulder. Once outside, the harridan motioned him to let her go on ahead; he dawdled, letting her get a good start, then trudged along behind her, around the corner and down a street to where a main thoroughfare pushed its way through the mean quarter of the town in which they were. Then she stopped, waited for him to come up, and hooked her arm in his; they walked on quickly, Coward's rucksack bumping against his legs. They continued for some distance along a fairly busy street, then he felt his arm tugged as she turned to mount the steps of an impressive building. In front of them was a brightly lit doorway, and answering her smile Coward allowed himself to be led inside. The hall seemed rather austere for such a large block of flats, but before he had time to ponder this he had been shown into a ground floor room and found himself gazing at a score or more policemen.

To the mustached official at a long desk the woman said simply:

"Hier ist ein Kriegsgefangener!"

Coward whirled around. Confronting him from just inside the door, a faint smile creasing his hatchet face, stood the man in the raincoat.

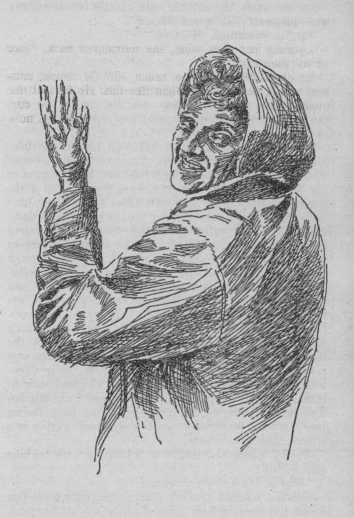

"Christ Almighty," he exploded. "A bloody police station!"

The barrel of a pistol covered him from the other side of the desk. He turned angrily to the woman, but she was already on her way out.

"Sorry, sweetheart," she said softly.

Surprisingly, the police were quite decent to him. He enjoyed a bowl of hot soup and a hunk of dry bread, then, wrapping himself in three blankets, settled down for the night in a fairly warm cell, sharing this luxury with a Viennese gentleman who had managed to get gloriously drunk. The policemen's questioning had been brief and to the point. It had been a short trip this time, he reflected ruefully, but well worth it; at least the ending had been less painful than the last.

In a mere two days he was back at Lamsdorf and once more stood before the adjutant, staring obstinately into that worthy's red and gloating features. Through the omnipresent interpreter, the German remarked:

"Not again, Mr. Coward? Good treatment this time, eh?"

He agreed cordially. "Very nice trip. Saw a lot of lovely country—might spend my holidays here after the war if I can get over the smell. And I was entertained most hospitably—I think your police force is wonderful, straight I do!"

This took a little time to sink in after it had been diplomatically translated.

"You'll have a nice long rest here this time, I can promise you, Mr. Coward. But first you will do one month in solitary confinement and I shall be most interested to see you wriggle out of that."

Later, when he had served his time in the cooler, he learned that the episode had very definitely had a bright lining. Of the fifteen men who had escaped from Stadt-Bau, no less than three had evaded recapture and might by now be well on the way to making home runs. Twenty per cent was a very nice average, he thought. Very nice indeed.

10

THE FOURTH YEAR

The fourth year of war rolled on. For the Allies 1943 was a period of materializing hopes, for it signaled the turning of the tide. On all sides their forces were slowly but surely obtaining leverage in their thrusts against the enemy, and the vast productive capacity of the United States had begun to exert its full and terrible pressure on the course of events.

In Africa the Germans fell steadily back to the west, yielding to the weight of Montgomery's Eighth Army while fighting grimly to preserve their lifeline across the Mediterranean. On the Russian front Hitler's armies found themselves, in conditions scarcely tolerable by the human body, grappling with an adversary of seemingly inexhaustible numbers; the German machine received blows that seriously undermined its strength and efficiency.

In the central European theatre, too, the R.A.F. had intensified its attack on the industrial potential of Germany. Recovering from its heavy losses of the previous year, the R.A.F. completely found its feet; the large-scale introduction of the Lancaster bomber began a battle in the night skies that grew inexorably heavier and mightier until it culminated, in synchronization with the desperate and never-easing struggles on land and sea, with the utter collapse of the enemy three years later. The Mosquito light bomber brought Berlin itself into the battle line, much to the satisfaction of the people of England's many smashed cities, who, though not particularly bloodthirsty by nature, recognized that the Germans were reaping their own rich

harvest. And as the Allied air offense gained momentum, the bombing of Britain by the *Luftwaffe* decreased until their raids were spasmodic and of relatively light striking power. Strengthened by the weight of American men and arms in Europe, while in the enormous expanses of the Pacific the Americans conducted their own terrible fight to the death with the Japanese, the Allies could see the first heartening glimpses of victory.

But while the tides of battle ebbed and flowed, appearing at times to engulf almost the entire world, small islands remained upon which were cast flotsam of humanity called prisoners of war. They comprised quite a large population and although somewhat thrust aside by the great powers themselves, formed a very important nucleus of men who had the time and opportunity to think and plan for the better days to come. England held many thousands of German and Italian prisoners, some being sent to Canada and the United States, but in Germany and the occupied countries were the unfortunates in greatest number. There, nearly two hundred thousand Britishers, hundreds of thousands of Frenchmen, thousands of Poles, Dutchmen, Hungarians, Czechs, Belgians, and something like three million Russians and Ukrainians dragged out their existence behind wire. This tremendous body of men worked in the main for their keep and had no option but to do so, especially those whose home countries did not subscribe to the Red Cross organization and were therefore destitute of any rights or privileges. But it can safely be said that the overwhelming majority of those who worked did so very badly, making as much trouble as they could for their captors; especially was this true of the British element, an ever-present burr in the vests of the Germans.

These thousands upon thousands of prisoners had to be fed and guarded. They were fed after a fashion; so meagerly in fact that but for the supply of Red Cross parcels, the non-working prisoners could never have survived the war. But guarded they were, and guarded well. This meant a constant drain of German soldiers from the fronts, a containing of useful forces: the Germans soon discovered that if they relaxed their vigilance no matter how slightly, the accursed Britishers would be off, requiring the time of hundreds of men to search for them.

The British element was split into camps, each one generally containing men from the same arm of service, with the officers in special *lagers* where certain privileges were permitted. Lamsdorf comprised some twelve thousand British Army men and a small contingent of about nine hundred from the R.A.F. Although presenting solid ranks to the hated "goon" (as the German guard became known), when by themselves they tended to break up into various groups, all quite harmless but providing the necessary stimulus and rivalry without which life would have been insufferably dull. Main groups were of nationalities and within these smaller loyalties grew. Among the English, for instance, there blossomed such societies as the Geordies, the West Countrymen, the East Enders, and so on. Some of the groups live on to this day in the guise of Old Comrade associations and Friendly Clubs the world over. Coward belonged to the Londoners' Club at Lamsdorf, but was restricted from taking a very active part in it because of his frequent excursions to the outside of the wire and his subsequent sojourns in the cooler.

It was a good year as years go when one is prisoner. Twice more Coward went out on working parties and twice more he escaped, only to be brought back after a few days and consigned to the cooler. The year was nearing its close when the order came for Coward to prepare for a third working party; told to be ready in half an hour, he could have had no inkling that this was to be an assignment outweighing all others in importance, with repercussions that were to be hotly debated by a battery of lawyers in postwar courtrooms and reported in the newspapers of many countries.

The name of the station, not far away, where he alighted to take charge of the party, rang a faint bell in his mind, though he could not recall at first just where he had heard it. He looked about him. Leading off from the platform was a large stockade such as is sometimes seen at country stations where cattle are herded to await the arrival of a goods train. He gave it hardly a second glance.

The station proved to be actually inside an enormous camp surrounding a new factory. Long rows of huts stretched out on either side of a rough rutted road; at the end of the road he could dimly see a concrete building with high chimneys. They were smoking heavily, sending thick black smoke rolling over the frozen countryside and tainting the air.

"Kommen Sie schnell!" shouted one of the guards and he moved forward again, following them out of the gates and along to the British camp some miles away. Later, seated on a form in the search hut, he pondered on the forbidding aspect of his new home. There certainly seemed little enough chance here to do anything. That shocking smell, polluting everything: what on earth were they burning? Rubber, was it? No, that was quite different. Chemicals, perhaps.

A guard had almost finished inspecting the contents of his pack emptied on to the floor, and was straightening up.

Coward asked him, "What's this place, Fritz?"

The man looked at him blankly.

"Auschwitz," persisted Coward. "This is Auschwitz isn't it?"

The man made as if to speak, then changed his mind. Expressionless, he nodded and turned away.

11

AUSCHWITZ

It was a small town, lying on the marshy ground between the River Vistula and the River Sola in Upper Silesia. Until the last war it had remained as anonymous as only a small farming community can, and would have never changed had not the German authorities noticed that during the First World War an Austrian cavalry camp had stood just outside the town. This camp, then in a state of utter disrepair, they renovated and enlarged, until it held some thousands of Russian prisoners. These poor men, treated worse than beasts of burden usually are, were there for one specific purpose: to construct the camp that was to become, in the eyes of the world, synonymous with hell. Next to the camp rose the huge buna factory, an industrial plant reputed to be one of the most modern in Europe for the production of synthetic oil and rubber, but since exposed as a center of bestiality with scarcely an equal in the history of mankind. Figures for the production of synthetics there have never come to light, but other figures, incredible in their proportions, are recorded, and they are figures of death. For it is now known that the primary purpose of the enormous factory was to assist in the rapid and complete extermination of European Jews and other unwanted foreign elements. This was the policy so coldly calculated for the liquidation of the Jewish race, including, of course, the confiscation of all property belonging to them and leading to the eventual "purification" of Aryan blood in the Greater Reich.

It is known that in June 1941, Himmler detailed Lieut. Col. Rudolf Hoess to organize the factory and camp with these ends in view, and to become its *Kommandant,* a post he accepted gratefully, carrying out his duties with vigor and enthusiasm. For a long time he was assisted by Kramer, a name that will forever strike a chill in the hearts of the comparative few who survived his ministrations; Kramer was to achieve notoriety as the "Beast of Belsen," an appellation that accurately typified the character of a mass murderer and torturer who seemed hardly of normal flesh and blood.

Hoess acquitted himself nobly at Auschwitz and at the end of 1941 the first consignments of Jews had begun to pour into the camp. First attempts at incineration were disappointing. The output from the gas chambers proved too big for the crude body-burning ovens to cope with. However, ingenuity was never lacking at Auschwitz. Early in 1942 a completely new system was adopted and several new, improved ovens were built, their lofty chimneys rearing into the sky to project their dreadful pollution across the now-German countryside. It may seem strange that the rolling black smoke failed to act as a stain on the German honor.

Three miles from the main factory and camp lay the small village of Monowitz; in it was the British camp, also built by the Russian labor. It was said that of the twelve hundred laborers, fewer than five hundred survived for other work. At Christmas, 1943, the camp held several hundred British prisoners employed in or near the buna factory; at that time they were engaged in digging trenches for electric cables and delayed the work as much as possible without exciting the trigger-finger of a guard. They had all been at Auschwitz for some time and differed from the usual crowd of prisoners of war: something of the general hopelessness of the area had them in its grip; they went about life quietly and with resignation. They would not have been Britishers had they not taken their pleasures seriously and in their off-time they organized sports as usual. But on the whole they were men who had seen dreadful things and showed it in their eyes.

Coward noticed this directly he arrived. He had a little room of sacking and wood in a corner of a barrack hut, and here he set up his diminutive office and worked with his indefatigable assistant, David Innes. The previous sergeant major in charge of the men had been returned sick to Lamsdorf, but although the fellows had been sorry to see him go, they welcomed Coward with open arms. His name and reputation were not unknown to them; indeed, there were several men there who had been on his earlier working parties and knew him well.

On his first evening he called a meeting of hut leaders and others who knew a bit about things, and looked around at the unsmiling faces. He spoke to the first.

"Now let's see, you're Johnny, aren't you? From Scotland?"

The young Scot, tall and gangly, nodded in affirmation. Beside him, a tubby little man gave tongue.

"And I'm George Randall from Capetown, and this," indicating his neighbor, "is Ernie Livingstone from God knows where, some shack town in the Midlands—" dodging a kick from the aggrieved one, who growled "Birmingham" as if the voice came from his boots, "—and this is Ted Cockrell from down under, Bert Smith or Smudger, from London, and the last but not least 'Erb, our 'Erb from Margate on Sea."

A few more introductions were volunteered and Coward grinned his thanks.

"Right, now I know you all. You know me by now —I'm Charlie to my pals and 'hey, you' to everybody else." He paused to light a cigarette, then looked up sharply. "Now look. I don't believe in beating about the bush and I hope you don't either. From what I've heard of things here, they're pretty grim. I don't mean the work we have to do, but the people you have to see and mix with. I shall know more about that once I

get out and about. But one thing I do know right now.
If we can't actually do any good ourselves we can do
our damnedest not to let things get us down and to
make the best of them until the boat sails. My information's probably later than yours and I can make a
guess that the boat won't be long." He hurried on before anyone could contradict. "In the first place I
propose to pep things up here as much as possible. I've
got more or less a free run and can go back to Lamsdorf for anything we need in the way of books, amuse-
ments, medicine and so on, and I can collect our
parcels from home. I'll have something to say if I can't
pull a wire here and there and wangle a few privileges
for the chaps. I believe in everyone pulling together; if
we do that no bastard can lick us. Agreed?"

"That's the way we see it," said Randall.

"Fine. We'll keep it that way. Now," he went on
more slowly, "having got that off my chest, there's one
thing more. I don't know what you blokes have been
doing about mucking up the working party side, but I
want to organize something really big if I can. Are
there any stooges here that you know of?"

Smudger scraped his jowls dubiously.

"Come on, now," said Coward, "are there, or aren't
there? I don't have to remind you that a stooge is just
as much your enemy as the guard outside, in fact more
so, because he's a spy."

"Well, Mr. Coward—" began Smudger.

"For crying out loud—Charlie."

Smudger grinned. "Well, Charlie, that's one thing we
meant to keep quiet about for a time. Still, we know
who you are now and I don't mind telling you we've got
a bloke here we think's a Jerry. Says his handle is
Miller and he comes from Durham. Supposed to be
in the Green Howards but none of the chaps here
from that mob have ever heard of him. We're pretty
sure he's been planted."

"How long has he been here?" asked Coward sharply.

"Came three weeks ago, by himself, from Lamsdorf."

"H'm. I'll check up on outgoing personnel the next time I go back. If he's a pigeon it'll be a job for someone. Any butchers in this shower?"

Smudger grinned again. "I shouldn't wonder."

"Good. Until I find out for sure, be very careful what you say in front of him. And don't let him suspect we've got our eyes on him."

"Don't worry, we don't let him know much."

"Right. One of you chaps can point him out to me later on. Now I want you all to explain what kind of work you're on and we'll see what's the best way to gum up the show."

For several hours the discussion continued, examining plans for escape, evolving possible forms of sabotage, and playing the foundation for a system of working that would ensure the least results with the appearance of most work.

The next day Coward marched his men through the village to where the great buna factory sprawled at the end of the road. It had still only reached about a quarter of its potential capacity, the electricity supply requiring further transformers. Beside the factory was a brand new camp of spotless-looking barracks.

"They're the Jerry staff quarters," said Smudger. "Do them proud, don't they? Almost fit for human habitation."

Under the watch of a number of toughly proportioned guards, they tramped around the outside of the wire and were soon put to work digging cable trenches. The day was bitterly cold; it was a relief to work if only to stimulate the blood and bring feeling back to the frozen feet. Coward, who had a fair measure of freedom, being the British Man of Confidence and therefore on a kind of parole, nodded to the *Unteroffizier* in charge and strolled away to spy out the land. He knew his urge to escape would have to be crushed at Auschwitz. These men needed someone to look after their interests; to do that he would have to remain with them, helping others to get away if possible, but never going himself. This was a position shared by several sergeant majors and officers in prison camps and was a yoke to be borne cheerfully, if with annoyance, for once let a trusted Man of Confidence attempt to escape and the Germans would immediately stop the come-and-go liaison between the big working parties and the main camp, and many of the men's little comforts and reliefs would disappear.

He walked slowly around the outside of the huge factory, taking in the scene. It was such that at first he could scarcely comprehend what he saw. Between the buildings great gangs of men and women labored, unseeingly, almost unknowingly, with dull eyes and blackened teeth, their only dress a suit of filthy dirty, pyjamalike material. It was obvious that their spindle bodies had ceased to react to cold and hunger. The weakness that occasionally overcame them was the only thing that seemed to bore into their torpidness and alarm them; when one of them staggered or fell he would glance fearfully behind him, and for a reason quickly apparent.

Over each gang of Jews, for such was their misfortune, was an overseer, or *kapo,* also a Jew but better dressed than the others. Usually he carried a large whip, which was put to use at least once every minute (some *kapos* preferred pieces of rope or bludgeons). All were characterized by brutality and an excess of energy with which they literally battered the life out of their less fortunate comrades. Afterward Coward found out that the *kapos* were promoted from the main gang on account of good work or toadying to the Germans; in their new position, holding the right of life or death over their fellows, they enjoyed a bunk to themselves in the barracks and could steal extra food with impunity from those under them. Coward felt his hackles rise as he watched, and gritted his teeth to prevent himself from crying out to these animals who defiled the human race with their lust to inflict pain. He could not know that the *kapos* were merely the product of the system. The men above them, the brains of the whole organization, bore the blame for their brutalization and for far worse things. Coward's education was just beginning.

He was about to turn away when in one of the gangs beside the wire a man fell to the ground. From where he stood Coward could see clearly that the creature was blue with cold and so thin that his bones protruded through the thin suiting, giving a grim travesty of some ghastly form of Victorian swimming costume. The *kapo* of the party strode up and with one blow from a stick laid the poor devil's head open to the bone. He looked hard at the man on the ground and smirked.

He called to his men. *"Wegtragen!"*

Two men came forward and heaved the body away, the broken head lolling from side to side, the arms hanging down straight, thin as sticks. He had been worked practically to death and then finished off with a truncheon; scarcely a drop of blood had been spilled.

The shock had been great, but Coward was to see much more of the same thing. The incident he had witnessed, happening before the gaze of a dozen German guards and civilians, was repeated every day and many times a day. For this was the plan of the Master Race. Don't just exterminate the Jews: that would mean spending good money on building gas chambers and furnaces with no return. First get your Jew, work him on practically no food, keep on working him until every ounce of energy and life has been drained from his body, and when he falls—poof! throw him in the gas chamber. There are plenty more.

Coward went back to his men at dinnertime and found them eating thin soup and odds and ends of parcel food. He took his share of the soup—a tempting concoction of swede and horsefat—and tried to eat, but he could not. From the men he elicited further information about conditions of work at the site and the general state of things in the factory. Bad as was the treatment of British prisoners, it was immeasurably better than that accorded to the slaves at Auschwitz; in fact, there could be no comparison. The Britishers' day's work ended at six, when they were marched back to camp and there had another meal consisting of potatoes and more soup, with eight hundred grams of bread and sometimes jam or margarine. These were heavy workers' rations and were not too bad when the Red Cross food was added. The diet did enable the men to remain tolerably fit, and their health was not unduly taxed by overwork for their German masters.

For the Jews and other slave workers, however, conditions were very different. Their working hours began at about six in the morning and lasted until six at night, or the same hours on a night shift. For this they were allowed about a pint of beans or *kraut* soup and three hundred grams of bread a day. Life would have been hard enough to maintain with no work to do, but on that meager amount of food the Jews were expected to work extremely hard throughout a twelve-hour day at the most exacting and rigorous jobs, clad in nothing but a pair of thin pyjamas and wooden clogs. The plan was deliberately contrived to wear them down and kill them off in the shortest space of time.

With the work, the lack of food, clothes, medicine, or sleeping accommodation fit even for cattle, and the sadistic flogging by the *kapos,* it was an unusual Jew who could survive for many weeks. The average expectancy of life was forty days; then his scarred, emaciated body was stripped by the *Sonderkommandos* inside the gas chamber and dumped on the trucks that ran on rails straight to the furnaces. Figures are not, and probably never will be, available on the precise number of Jews who passed to their death through the Auschwitz factory, controlled with conveyor-belt efficiency by the I. G. Farben industrial combine, but some idea of the scale of extermination can be gathered from the fact that Hoess, *Kommandant* of the camp from 1941 to 1945, openly boasted at his war crimes trial that he had been responsible for the murders of over two and a half million Jews.

That evening, back in the barracks, Coward began to plan to rob the Germans of at least a few of their victims. He had learned that most of the Jews who arrived at the buna camp were in such a state of misery

that their fatalism had robbed them of any will to help
themselves. With all reasoning apparently dead, they
allowed themselves to be herded along by a few guards
to the concentration camps, when a determined effort
by the majority would have provided a chance for at
least a few of them to escape. But among the acquies-
cent thousands, suffering without protest the ageless
persecution of their race, there were inevitable excep-
tions. Jews captured from the professional classes,
lawyers, doctors or businessmen, did sometimes show a
spark of initiative and attempt to escape. Some did a
good job of sabotage while at work; some tried to rouse
their comrades to rebellion, even to death, against
the guards. It was to these men that Coward decided
to appeal. He would try to offer a chance of escape,
encouraging them meanwhile in sabotage. He sat rack-
ing his brains. Some fairly foolproof plan must be hit
on to extract these people from the camp and get them
into the outside world, giving them some chance,
however slender, of reaching a neutral country or, at
worst, of ending their lives quickly in an attempt to
live. Come what may, he had to salve his own conscience as a human being by giving them the opportunity to cry quits.

As he was preparing for bed, just before lights-out
at ten, Smudger came into his cubicle and perched on
the edge of his bunk.

"Will you be able to go into town tomorrow, Charlie?" he asked.

Coward looked at him quizzically and smiled.

"Nothing but a bloody errand boy here, eh?"

" 'Course you are," returned Smudger. "That's the
only bleedin' use of you W.O.'s on these camps."

They chuckled and Smudger offered a cigarette.

"Well," said Coward, exhaling noisily, "at least I'm
some use then, which is more than I can say for you."
In his mind stretched a vista of months of useful work
for the lads, with buying expeditions that were certainly
welcome reliefs from the camp, but which bound him
on his honor not to escape. It was not an encouraging
prospect. "Yes, I might as well go. I want to get out

as much as I can and it's a good excuse if you boys want any fag-papers or matches."

"Here you are, then—the list and the money. We generally want things about once a week—pencils, razor blades, and such like. If you go into Winkler's shop in the High Street and ask him for English tobacco he'll give you—"

"Blimey, not half a pound of Cut Bar?"

"Where d'you think you are—back in London? No, he'll give you a bottle of *schnapps*. The boys want a drink tonight."

"*Schnapps,* eh! So that's the way the land lies, is it? I wouldn't say no to a drink myself. Is it good?"

"Not bad. Made from sour apples, I think. Anyway, it's the real McCoy all right."

"Okay, I'll get it, Smudge, and the rest of the things. Anything else?"

Smudge stood up and eyed him.

"Look, Charlie," he said. "I've just been jawing with old Hans, the postern outside the main gate. There's another barrowload of Jews, poor devils, arriving tomorrow morning. If you want to see something that'll really shake you, you ought to be in on that. You ain't seen nothing yet, believe me."

"Thanks for the tip, Smudge. I'll try to be there."

12

THE SPY

Clerical work kept him occupied the next morning. It was a task demanding a combination of tact, craft and cunning. The idea at all British working camps was to keep the maximum number of unemployed, resulting in the men being literally encouraged by their N.C.O.s to report sick at the slightest excuse; this reversal of normal service procedure caused many laughs. Even if the German *Stabsarzt,* a kind of unregistered army doctor, told them they were not sick and must return to work, several precious hours had been wasted. Coward found that a regular roster was maintained at Monowitz for men going sick and although it was broken up a little to avoid suspicion, a steady stream of colds, toothaches, mysterious muscular pains and "itises" of all descriptions flowed through his hands. Whenever any man fell genuinely ill he was sent back to Lamsdorf for treatment there by British doctors.

Coward chuckled as he went through the list, marking off the complaint against each man's name. He looked up as one of them whose turn it was to report sick that morning came into the room.

"What-ho, chum," he greeted him. "Let's see, what are you down for—a pain in the side?"

"That's right, brother. Clatterbridge is the name." The tall, thin individual sat down, and Coward eyed him curiously. He had heard of Clatterbridge. The man was reputed to be a religious maniac, not quite "all there," although all the men treated him with the utmost civility and respect. The life of a prisoner frequently warped the mind into strange shapes; most of the prisoners turned instinctively to the Church for solace in their hardships, but just a few went too far and became slightly unhinged. This man had made rather a nuisance of himself by attempting to convert everyone at hand, but after some forcible arguments (emphasized by the toes of several boots) had desisted and withdrawn into a private shell from which he emerged only to go to work and to eat. Even now he produced a bible from his pocket and began to read. He was a good man and although Coward knew only part of his story he felt moved by his obvious devotion.

After a short spell of reading, Clatterbridge looked up.

"By the way, S'arnt major," he said, "the next time you go into Berkenwald would you do me a favor?"

"That's the little town this side of Auschwitz itself, isn't it? Sure, son, what d'you want?"

"I should be much obliged if you would visit the optician's there and change these glasses for me. The other Man of Confidence got them for me but they never suited and I didn't like to tell him after all his trouble. Would you mind? Tell the man I want them stronger."

Coward was touched. "Of course. I'll let you know when I'm going and get those glasses off you."

Clatterbridge paused, as if making up his mind.

"When you go, brother," he continued, in his curiously high, rasping voice, "ask the man for some polishing rags for the specs, will you? I think you'll like those polishing rags." He chuckled throatily. "The other s'arnt major had quite a few off him and put them under a floorboard here."

Coward stared at him in bewilderment.

"Polishing rags?" he echoed blankly. "Put polishing rags under the floor? What on earth for?"

Clatterbridge leaned forward, the light in his eyes not quite as mild as Coward would have wished.

"Why don't you have a look for yourself?"

Coward scraped back his wooden form and stood up.

"Now look here, old chap—" he began, but the tall
soldier was already rummaging in the corner under the
bunk, straining at the floorboards and hissing slightly
through his teeth as he pulled. Suddenly, in front of
Coward's startled eyes, a floorboard slid out, so smoothly that he knew it must have been grooved. Clatterbridge thrust his arm into the hole and lifted out one,
two, three, and then four automatic pistols, laying
them down side by side, gleaming and deadly, on
the floor. Coward could only gape and stammer.

"There are also," continued Clatterbridge, "two doz-
en clips of ammunition and a hand grenade."

"A hand grenade?" Coward sat down weakly on the
table and drew heavily on his cigarette. "But for Pete's
sake—are those the polishing rags you were burbling
about?"

The other grinned. "Naturally, brother. They are the
tools with which we shall destroy the Antichrist. With
these we shall play our part in the cleansing of this
sad world. We shall rid it of the unclean, unchristian
German."

"Just a minute," cut in Coward excitedly. "You say
you got these from an optician's in Berkenwald?" He
picked up a revolver and examined it. "How much
did you pay for them? What's the catch?"

"They don't cost a penny. Someone he knows steals
them from German army stores at Breslau and
smuggles them here."

"Well, get them away quickly before someone
comes."

As the guns were replaced, Coward sat and let his
mind race with possibilities. He saw an armed uprising
of Jews fighting their way out of bondage, beating
their path to the frontiers and peace. Then he sighed;
it would never work. Clatterbridge stood up again,
watching him closely. He broke the silence with another conversational bomb that made Coward jump.

"Of course, if he could get hold of the dynamite, we
could do some real good."

"Dynamite!"

"He was trying to get it. The other s'arnt-major and

I were in his shop once; he was measuring me for glasses when he spoke about it. The army camp would look grand with a few charges exploding under it."

"Damn the army camp," roared Coward. "It's the buna factory I'd like to see go up."

"No, no," reproved Clatterbridge sternly. "It is the Anti-christ we must exterminate. Believe me, brother, we shall indeed be welcome in heaven if we can wipe this scourge off the face of the earth."

Coward hurriedly agreed, not wanting to annoy him at this juncture. "You're perfectly right," he said. "I'll get down to that shop as soon as I can."

"Hush—"

The door opened and in stamped the German *Stabsarzt,* puffing and blowing and complaining bitterly of the walk over from Berkenwald. Coward was amazed by the look of sheer hatred that Clatterbridge gave the German. His was a dangerous form of lunacy, apparently demanding the death of all Germans. He would have to be watched carefully in case he tried to start his own private war and got hurt in the attempt. Coward knew very well that to use the weapons themselves would be certain suicide. No, the best idea would be to give them to the Jews inside the camp at Auschwitz so they could attempt a mass break or at least die fighting, taking with them as many Germans as they could. He resolved to contact the optician without delay. Meanwhile, Clatterbridge's pain in the side was quickly disposed of and he was despatched with a guard to rejoin his companions at the Auschwitz digging site.

Once again that evening, when Coward prepared to turn in for bed, he congratulated himself that a fair day's work lay behind him. The expected consignment of Jews had not yet arrived, but he felt thankful for that. In addition, he had stumbled on a vitally important secret, one that opened up magnificent opportunities. Just before the lights were turned off at the mains, he caught a glimpse of Clatterbridge. The bloodthirsty man of God was upended on his blanket spread over the cold floor. He was praying almost upside down, in Eastern fashion. Who can say what personal god or gods listened to his entreaties? That he derived comfort from his supplications was enough.

Tragedy struck the next day, suddenly and without warning. Coward had marched down with the men to the site outside the wire of the buna factory and stood there chatting with some of them as they prepared for the day's toil. A hefty *Unteroffizier* moved slowly up and down the ranks, growling at them to begin work. Reluctantly, the men started, some digging, some shaping the ditches and shoring them with planks, some manhandling large cable drums. At the foot of a newly-erected pylon a little group gathered, arguing. Coward walked over to see what the trouble was about; as he approached he was joined by the *Unteroffizier,* a sullen lout well known by the working party for his ferocity.

"Die Verfluchten Engländer," muttered the German to Coward. "They are lazy pigs. I will make them work —you will see."

Coward said clearly, "You lay a hand on one of those men and there'll be trouble, *Unteroffizier."*

The man sneered back and elbowed his way into the men. Three Britishers, one of them a young English corporal named Reynolds, were angrily refusing to climb the steel pylon in that cold weather unless they had rubber boots and sufficiently thick gloves. A German private bawled at them to start climbing, and fast. The *Unteroffizier* added the weight of his bellow.

"Climb! Climb! *Raus,* pig-dogs! I will shoot!"

Reynolds turned a white face to Coward

"For God's sake," he appealed. "We're supposed to climb this thing to fix cables without proper gloves or climbing kit. In this weather, too. It's suicide to go up without them, and I'm damned if I'm going."

"Climb!" shrieked the *Unteroffizier.* "Climb!"

Reynolds shrugged. "I'm going back to the other chaps," he said quietly.

"Watch it," warned Coward. "I don't like the look of this rat—he's dangerous."

The corporal laughed grimly. "It's only bluster. He wouldn't dare."

He began to walk away from the group; Coward saw a pistol appear in the German's hand and shouted "Look out, man!"

Reynolds turned and stared with open mouth as the gun thundered. He stood quite still for a moment, a small dark stain appearing on the breast of his khaki tunic. Then he cried, "Christ, he's shot me!" and crumpled in a heap on the frozen ground.

The Britishers rushed forward to where he lay, but he was dead. Coward knelt beside him, then looked long as the *Unteroffizier* who now stood with the smoking pistol in his hand, clearly shaken by the results of his choler.

"You yellow, dirty swine," said Coward deliberately.

Quickly surrounding the body, the German guards let no one near until a doctor had been summoned and pronounced the man dead. The Britishers stood in shocked groups, heedless of the shouts of the guards to recommence work. A great anger possessed them all. Poor Reynolds had been a gentle man, popular with all his comrades. To such a man the cold-blooded murder of a defenseless prisoner would have seemed inconceivable. But he underestimated his captors and had paid totally for his protest. Some of the men, remembering what he was and how he had lived, said a simple prayer for him in the corner of the field. Coward stood unseeing through the humble offering, utterly choked.

In due course the men were allowed to carry the body into a nearby barn; there it lay until a rude coffin had been made at the town of Auschwitz. Two days later it was lifted on to a cart for burial in an adjacent cemetery. The entire working party, their mixture of uniforms achieving an astonishing smartness for the occasion, paraded and followed Coward as he led the pallbearers to the last resting place. A Union Jack draped the coffin, infusing the ceremony, so renderingly personal to all present, with the dignity of a soldier's grave.

Accompanied by a guard, Coward returned immediately to Lamsdorf, ostensibly to collect letters and parcels but really to report the murder to the British authorities via R.S.M. Sheriffs, together with the name of the *Unteroffizier* who was responsible. He also wrote the details to his wife, suitably camouflaged in a code he had used the previous year and which had evolved as a result of his escape to Ulm. He had wanted to complain officially of several things and had sent a letter, worded as if talking of family matters, addressed to "Charles Coward Snr., c/o William Orange" at his own home in London. The surprise of Mrs. Coward was great—indeed, when, in reference to the strange missiles he chanced upon and which later proved to be the dreaded V.1's, the first guided missiles, she read ob-

scure descriptions of birds and bees, she began to fear
for her husband's sanity. Then she realized that William
Orange, a gentleman of whom she had never heard,
must be none other than the War Office. So Coward's
messages reached their destination; he followed the
method consistently and after the war M.1.9. acknowledged his excellent work in an official commendation.

Having thus done his duty to the dead soldier he
visited some of his old Lamsdorf pals and enjoyed a
yarn. While there he checked on the suspected stooge
at Auschwitz, finding that the men's doubts were justi-
fied. No man by the name of Miller had been sent to
join the Auschwitz working party: conclusive proof
that he was a German "plant." Coward's lips tightened
as he heard this news; he mentally repeated the gypsy
injunction, "An eye for an eye." One man had died,
killed treacherously by a German. Now a German
must die. It would be rough justice.

Returning to Auschwitz, he approached the town in
the rickety old train with a thrill of anticipation. Soon
things were going to hum in the factory, he hoped. He
was so cheered by the thought of Clatterbridge's supply
of arms that he felt positively benign and offered his
guard a cigarette with an air of lordly benevolence.
The man accepted it gratefully and began to talk: Coward found the staccato rattle of remarks difficult to
understand, but gathered that the German people were
sick and tired of war and all its suffering. The guard
had lost his home in Hamburg to the bombs of the
R.A.F. and had arrived on leave to find his father
killed and his family evacuated to Dresden.

Coward nodded sympathetically, but his mood un-
derwent an instant change when the train drew in at
Auschwitz. The expected Jewish draft had just come; a
long train of box cars was standing at the platform and
thousands of miserable creatures were making their
way down ramps into the stockade. Coward stood with
the German guard and watched, his heart sick within
him. The compound was certainly for cattle, but human cattle.

Before him waited a great sea of filthy, undressed

Jews in all stages of emaciation and privation. It was impossible to guess how long their train had been held up on its journey but the toll in human life was only too evident in the pile of bodies stacked on the platform. There lay men, women and children, awaiting the final degradation of the carts to bear their remains to the furnaces.

Attached to the large compound was a smaller one, and in it stood a group of Germans. Among them was a *Stabsarzt,* several army officers, a Gestapo agent and a number of civilians: the civilians, Coward's guard explained, were comprised of local farmers and the managers of the buna factory. A trickle of Jews passed from the *lager* into the smaller compound, kicked and hustled by the soldiers attending them. The Germans looked them over. The stronger looking men and children were motioned to stand to one side by the farmers and periodically herded out to waiting carts. Others, of both sexes and including older children, who were at least standing fairly erect, were selected for the factory; one of the managers consulted from time to time a sheet of paper in his hand, as if checking the numbers required. The factory workers were marched outside and lined up on the road leading to the main camp.

The guard shrugged.

Eventually about a thousand remained, old men and women or younger women carrying children.

"What happens to those?" asked Coward.

The guard shrugged.

"Tod," he said. "Death."

Appalled, Coward struggled to assimilate the fact. God in heaven, were these poor wretches to be butchered in cold blood? The guard pointed along the road. In the distance could be seen the long building with the white concrete roof that Coward knew were the gas chambers. Evidently this consignment were not to await their turn at the working camp. Already people were filing past, some stumbling in their exhaustion, some walking firmly, but all on their way to death.

Coward insisted that his guard take him a little way along the road, until he could clearly see the entrance to the chambers. Before the building was a gate and on reaching this the Jews were ordered to remove all their clothing. Old men with thin matchstick legs stood in the icy air convulsed with trembling; several women fell into the snow and were heaved up by their friends or relations. Coward saw one young girl, naked and marble white with the cold, clutching a child of a few months to her breast while the infant attempted to extract some nourishment from her pathetic body. She led by the hand a small girl of about five, crooning a song as she went along. The song became louder as she entered the gate of the death house; it was taken up by others and despite the kicks and blows aimed by the guards swelled in volume until it assumed the last gesture of this proud race. The Jews seemed to walk strongly once more, ignoring their grotesque nakedness. They steadied themselves, the infants ceased whimpering, and in their song they became again the Children of God, marching to their last Canaan.

Coward watched as the gates closed behind them and the song grew fainter. He was conscious of a feeling of pride that men and women could bear themselves to their doom with such courage. Their religion was not his, to be sure, but they typified the eternal values, so elusive to define yet so overwhelmingly right when demonstrated in the face of unimaginable disaster.

It was with no sense of pity or shame, but rather one of considerable satisfaction, that he gathered the camp leaders together in the evening and confirmed their suspicions of the stooge. He noticed the men's faces harden in the dull light from the swinging electric bulb and hoped that the die was cast.

He was not disappointed. At the next morning's roll call one man was missing, the level in the cesspool just a little higher.

13

THE PHOTOGRAPHER'S SHOP

Early in March the opportunity came for him to investigate Clatterbridge's scheme. By then the plan for arming some of the Jews had taken definite shape in his mind; whatever the outcome of a mass attempt to escape, the fact that they would be able to repay favors to at least a few of the Germans was a delicious prospect. But he would have to act carefully. A brawny guard had been detailed to accompany him when he went abroad on his business and with the German constantly present it was a ticklish job to smuggle anything into the camp; to bring arms through into the barracks would be a brainteaser indeed.

He decided first to spy out the land and to this end informed the guard that he wanted to go into nearby Berkenwald to have his eyes tested, and the German made no objection, assuming that his British charge had obtained permission from the *Stabsarzt*. They set out early and caught the bus that ran past the British camp at Monowitz, seating themselves among the country people going to work. For the purpose of short bus journeys Coward was allowed a certain amount of German money, as distinct from the camp *Lagergeld;* he paid their fares with calm indifference and waited for Berkenwald to show up, meanwhile inspecting his fellow travelers with interest.

They were the usual nondescript crowd of women and elderly peasants. No young men were to be seen except two soldiers: all those eligible had long since been called into the fighting services. Beside Coward sat a fat old *frau* who regarded him with undisguised contempt and did her best to push him off the seat with her capacious rump. Opposite sat a personable girl of about twenty, eyeing him as malevolently as all German girls eyed foreign prisoners; they all seemed to be trained to spit upon other nationalities, and this one was no exception. As the bus rattled to one of its stops she arose to alight, turning as she did so to launch a wad of spittle in Coward's direction. This mark of attention he had experienced many times before, but never so blatantly and publicly. He returned the compliment promptly in Anglo-Saxon and made to get to his feet but the hand of the guard restrained him. To his surprise, the big German private appeared to take the incident very much to heart; seizing the girl by the wrist he delivered a heated lecture of good manners and the decent treatment of prisoners of war. In this he was joined by the other two soldiers, who had been indignant spectators of the girl's conduct.

Eventually the postern released the girl, now fairly raging, and she flounced off, hurling insults after the bus as it moved away. Coward offered his cigarettes around to the soldiers, losing no opportunity of impressing on the severely rationed German population the superior conditions of British prisoners.

"Thanks, Fritz," he said to his guard. "That was decent of you."

The soldier shrugged and intimated that slips of girls could never get it into their stupid heads that the British were fighting men too, and that in any case many German brothers and husbands were held captive in England and in a similar plight.

"Well anyway, ta," repeated Coward chirpily. The German's attitude was interesting; perhaps he would be sufficiently sympathetic to wink his eye at any irregular goings-on. It was worth a try, although considerable care would be needed.

Slowly the bus ground past the entrance to the mighty buna works, the Auschwitz camps stretching behind them, turned along a road leading through the village and then down the main highway to Berkenwald. Rumbling into a square, it pulled up in front of a police station, a rough wooden building displaying notices of Jews who had escaped and reminding farmers that they could call on the camp for slave labor.

"This way," grunted the guard, who answered so well to the name of Fritz that it might well have been his name. He led Coward past a row of somewhat shabby looking shops remarkable for their empty windows, and at the extreme end of the street entered a dark, low-fronted establishment boasting a large sign in the shape of a balefully staring eye.

Inside, a small man came forward to meet them, peering at Coward through spectacles with lenses of astonishing thickness with magnified his eyes to nightmare proportions. Although of no great age, he was gray haired and seemed shorter than he really was by reason of a perpetual stoop. Fritz explained the purpose of their visit and seated himself with a magazine. The optician turned to Coward.

"*Kommen Sie mit, Herr Feldwebel,*" he murmured, motioning to an inner room. Coward found himself in a typical consulting room equipped with inspection glasses and letter charts.

"Do you speak English?" he asked.

If he heard the question, the optician ignored it. Donning a white coat, he signed to him to take a seat, and for ten minutes or so the only sounds were the clicking of the optician's lamp and Coward's recital of the reading cards. Then the lamp was clicked off, the light switched on, and the optician said quietly but abruptly:

"There is nothing wrong with your eyes, sergeant major."

Coward grinned. This was no news to him: to this day he has the eyesight of a lynx.

"There's nothing wrong with your English either, is there?" he returned affably.

A faint smile passed across the other's face.

"Thank you. I like to speak it when I can, but you understand it is very dangerous when a German is near."

Coward was surprised. "But aren't you a German?"

"I am Polish," replied the optician in almost a whisper, but with a smoldering deliberation. "The Germans are not my friends." He was silent for a moment, then asked, "But why do you come here when there is clearly nothing troubling your vision? What makes you think you need spectacles?"

Coward produced his cigarettes and offered one, wondering whether to take the plunge.

"What's your name?" he asked.

"You can call me Jan."

"Good. Mine's Coward, Charles Coward. Look, Jan, I believe you are able to get me certain materials that I want. Is that right?"

Jan made no sign. He looked calmly at Coward through a cloud of smoke and spat a shred of tobacco from his lips.

"Materials?" he repeated. "What materials?"

"I need a lot of polishing rags, all you can get."

"That is a strange request—polishing rags."

"I know you were able to supply some to the sergeant major before me at Monowitz. Will you help me, too?"

Jan stood up and crushed the lighted end from his cigarette, carefully placing the stump in his pocket. He accepted a full packet from Coward with a short bow.

"Polishing rags are in great demand and short supply," he said with a hint of a chuckle. "I fear I cannot help you at all. Such luxuries are hard to come by, and I do not know you."

"You can soon find out, can't you? I'll tell you anything you want to know, and I can supply you with plenty of cigarettes or tinned food for what I want. If you think I'm a Jerry stooge just ask the Germans at Lamsdorf about me—they'll tell you!"

Jan smiled deprecatingly and waved his hand.

"Sergeant major, may I offer you some advice? Sometimes it is ill-advised to rush headlong at one's objective." He paused. "Now let me see. Your pair of special spectacles will need several fittings. You had better come again in two weeks to see me."

Coward grabbed his hand, beaming. "Thanks, friend. I knew you would come up trumps."

"'Come up trumps'—I must remember that. No, don't rush away, Mr. Coward, or shall I call you Karl? Before your next visit may I suggest that you arrange for a photographer to take pictures of your men? I am sure their families at home would be pleased to have them."

Coward stared at him blankly, but he continued talking in his quiet voice and precise English.

"There is an excellent photographer, a Pole, in Auschwitz village. I suggest you engage his services. Tell him Jan sent you. You will not be disappointed." He opened the door to the waiting room. "In two weeks, then, for the first fitting. Look after that guard of yours," he added jocularly as the German rose. "He's a good fellow, but smokes too much."

He spoke rapidly to Fritz in German, explaining the necessity of further consultations; Fritz nodded and once more led the way into the street. Coward's brain worked fast as they walked back to the bus stop, reviewing what had happened and estimating how far he could push his luck. Impulsively, as they reached the queue waiting for the bus, he slipped a packet of twenty cigarettes into the German's hand. He had long ago found it essential to be well primed with this currency whenever on expeditions outside the camp. Money was of little use, but for cigarettes, soap and certain kinds of food the average German guard would sell his soul. Fritz, certainly not above average in such matters, accepted the gift with a bleak smile; when the bus arrived he ushered Coward on with something like deference.

"Listen, Fritz," said Coward against the rumble of the engine. "I want to get off at Auschwitz to go to the photographer's. D'you understand? Can we do that?"

"*Auschwitz? Jawohl.*"

"Yes, all the men want their pictures taken for their frauleins at home."

The shop in question proved to be a good deal smarter than its neighbors. Fritz conveyed that the

proprietor did a lot of work for the government and was very wealthy; the information was not encouraging, for he would be hard to bribe.

An attractive, dark-haired young woman greeted them from behind the counter. She smiled at Coward, making him somewhat uncomfortable: his dealings with women had been severely circumscribed during the past few years and he felt awkward and rough when confronted with them. He explained in very sparse German what he required and the girl invited him to inspect an album of group photographs. Glancing at Fritz, who lingered boredly in the doorway, she leaned forward, her scent wafting agreeably about her.

"Mr. Coward?" she asked softly.

He was startled, and she laughed quietly, showing beautifully white teeth.

"We heard from Jan," she murmured in good English. Then, louder, "You want some pictures taken of your men and yourself—we shall be happy, sergeant major. We do not have much film for such purposes, but perhaps we will find you some." He stuttered something about a visit to the camp, but she cut him off. "If you will come here in two days' time, we will arrange everything, yes? My husband will tell you then if we can be of service to you."

Coward realized suddenly that they intended to investigate him; when they found he was genuine the rest should be comparatively easy. Merely a matter of smuggling, with death as the probable penalty for any slip-up.

"Thanks," he managed to say, feeling partly elated at the established contact, and partly annoyed that the girl was married. "I'm sure everything will be all right. I'll be back in two days." He hesitated, undecided. "Er—if there's anything besides money—I mean—"

She laughed again. "Sergeant major, my husband and I are patriots and take only money for our work."

He caught the double meaning but tried again. "Or if you like a few cakes of soap—"

Her eyes softened. Soap was to her an unhea

luxury, used as she was to the ration issue of barely disguised pumice. "That would be very kind." The nearness of her began to wreak havoc with Coward's self-control. "Thank you," she breathed.

"That's fine. Goodbye, then," he said briskly, plunging out to rejoin Fritz, who stood staring bovinely at the smoking chimneys of Birkenau on the horizon. Coward looked too, and came down to earth with a jolt.

Even at that distance, fingers of flame were clearly visible at the tops of the chimneys, while smoke billowed lazily out on the faint breeze, carrying with it the sweetish, ever-present odor. The "bakery," as the grim building was known to the surrounding camps, appeared to be working at full pressure.

He shuddered, not the first time since arriving at Auschwitz and most assuredly not the last. Everything had the elements of a nightmare; the pleasant fields of England, the homely folk around their fires or queueing for the cinema or carrying out their wartime tasks with cheerful humor and cups of cocoa, seemed a thousand worlds away. How could they possibly know the character of their enemy, and if rumor of the horror of Auschwitz and other extermination centers leaked out to them, who could blame their disbelief of such seemingly crude and disgusting propaganda?

Coward was scarcely aware of the short bus journey back to Monowitz. He was startled when, on entering the camp, a voice broke in upon his lowering thoughts and he found himself accosted by the German officer in charge of working parties.

"Oh, sergeant major," came the wheedling tones of the little man. "I have a favor to ask, please."

Coward was in no mood to return the civility.

"You have, eh? Do me a favor too, will you?"

"Yes, yes, if possible."

"It's possible all right. Just go and—oh, never mind. What is it now?"

"A small thing. A little cooperation, yes?"

"Cooperation! Where'd you learn that word?"

"Ah, the sergeant major must his joke make, yes?

This afternoon, some of your men to work on the freight cars at the station. You will arrange?"

"Work on wagons? Did the last sergeant major allow that?"

"He was stupid man. The work was of no importance to our war effort. You know we never force you Britishers—"

"Oh no!"

"—but this time I appeal to you. Our labor at the station is short. We will give privileges."

"I know what you mean by privileges. One less bullet in the guts, eh?"

"No, no, Mr. Coward. We shall arrange special reward."

He reflected. It was common knowledge that the goods yards were the junction for that part of Lower Silesia, handling a high proportion of the traffic for Poland and the Russian and Italian fronts. Here, surely, were opportunities for a good party, and at least it would result in taking some prisoners off work at the buna factory for a day or so.

"All right," he said. "I'll get a squad of my men down there first thing tomorrow morning. How long will the job last?"

"Indefinitely. Report with your men and you will not find me ungrateful, Mr. Coward. The foreman will tell you what to do."

The officer strode away, obviously pleased with himself. So often did the damned Britishers insist on the letter of The Hague Convention and refuse to do anything directly useful to Germany's prosecution of the war. The *Hauptmann* would be delighted at the new sergeant major's easy capitulation.

As for Coward, he was equally contented. The marshalling yards should provide quite a frolic, although he was prepared to wager a year's Red Cross parcels that his lads would not be employed on the job "indefinitely."

14

UNDERGROUND ARMY

Coward's bet would have been safe enough, in all conscience. Directly after breakfast he led a party of about thirty strong to the marshalling yard that lay along the side of the buna plant. The natural reluctance of the men to help the enemy with the important job of getting the freight cars rolling for the warfronts of Europe had been overcome rather forcibly by his short address the evening before.

"Now get this into your heads. We're not going on this little outing because we need the exercise. It gives us an opportunity to have a quiet bash at the square-heads, but make it a quiet one. Don't do any obvious sabotage or we'll find ourselves against a wall. I mean, don't tear up the rails or any silly ass tricks like that. The things I want you to do are little jobs that show trouble later on, down the line. Bits of stone and sand in the axle boxes of the trucks, switching over the destination labels, loosening floorboards, making holes in the roofs of the cars, and so on. Remember that the essence of capers like this is that the damage doesn't show up until it's too late. Use your loafs and let's see what you can do."

His listeners were grinning broadly when they had finally retired to their bunks, and now walked with a will to the sidings, determined to put the plan into operation. The confusion that followed will probably provide a topic of conversation for German railway men for a long time to come. Everywhere on the German railways system, at that time, conditions were extremely difficult. Intent on his "guns before butter" schemes, Hitler had neglected one of the most vital factors in the prosecution of any war; that of the railways, the biggest single link in the transport system of the country and the most decisive one in the lines of supply. Consequently, little or no new rolling stock had been put on the roads for many years, and the permanent way itself was in poor and sometimes even dangerous condition. Under the enormous and sudden strain of total war, the railway system had faltered but somehow managed to carry on, mainly through the Herculean efforts of the railwaymen themselves. Then, in 1943 and more so in 1944, the Allied offensive had paid particular attention to the railways, and those same workers were faced not only with very hard labor and extremely long hours, but also with the strain of bombing and, what was dreaded even more, cannon shell attacks from fast-moving fighters. This meant that the system in Western Germany was very nearly defunct. Nearly all passenger trains were employed for troop movements, while the major part of such traffic as still existed consisted of essential goods. Bottlenecks arose at all the important junctions, making the use of prisoner labor practically inevitable to help sort out the jams.

The men marched into the yard at a swing, a mouth organ wheezing out the strains of "The British Grenadiers," until a sharp command brought them to a smart halt. This show had been previously thought up to impress the watching Germans with their bearing and efficiency and so make it less likely that any sabotage be traced home to them.

Coward bellowed "Stand easy!" and went in search of the *Unteroffizier* who was to direct the operation. The few German guards who had accompanied the Britishers stood dejectedly at ease, looking, as always, utterly scruffy and unkempt. They were in sharp contrast to the prisoners, some of whom wore the old type of army jacket and simply gleamed with polished brass.

Coward soon returned with both the *Unteroffizier* and the yard foreman, and the work commenced. The men were split up into gangs of five, some shunting with the help of a couple of smelly little locomotives, some checking wagons for loads and faults, others inspecting the lines and points and applying grease and spanners where necessary. The first day went off quite well: the foreman breathed a sigh of relief at the amount of work being done, and being done well to boot. Even the *Unteroffizier* relaxed a little and waxed affable to Coward over a cup of "coffee" in the fitters' cabin.

Life was sweet the next day as the men marched once more into the yard. But alas all the nuts that had been tightened were now unscrewed, grease was put on the sleepers and not on the points, wagons were inspected for faults with such enthusiasm that faults were introduced to enhance the job, and a hundred and one similar small occurrences took place. Coward himself spent a happy few hours each day for the next week or two, walking along the lines of trucks awaiting shunting to their respective trains, and changing over every destination card in the steel clip on the side of each wagon. A truck bearing a card consigning cement to Italy would suddenly change its load to that of guncotton for the Russian front. Once he sent a load of tinned meat to Holland instead of to the army in the frozen wastes of the Ukrainian Steppes: they got a few thousand tins of green paint in its place, and he hoped they found it sustaining.

The other men were hard at it, too. Hundreds of wagons were tampered with in one way or another, their weaknesses of age and hard service drastically encouraged. Wherever possible, their contents were spoiled by water or exposure. Tins were punctured, petrol tankers holed, couplings unscrewed to the last turn. In the two weeks for which the British contingent were on the job they must have caused untold damage to the railways and aimed quite an effective blow at the German war effort.

At the end of that time they were quietly withdrawn from the marshalling yard and, although no word of accusation or complaint was ever breathed, the German officer whose idea it had been to send them never spoke directly to Coward again, but issued his orders through a subordinate. He certainly never requested another favor. Coward had the impression that he was not trusted by the Germans; sad at the thought, and to revive his drooping spirits, he smuggled in a couple of bottles of *schnapps* and threw a little party for his men.

But the press of these hilarious days had not driven from his mind his appointment at the photographer's shop in Auschwitz. At the proper time he walked down to the village with Fritz looming beside him and reported to the woman behind the counter. She beamed, raising his pulse just one degree in doing so.

"Ah, sergeant major, will you come through?"

He glanced back at Fritz. The stolid German stood absently picking his teeth while inspecting the albums of sample photographs that littered the counter. He would be safe for a time. Coward reflected, and patted the cake of soap and fifty cigarettes in his pocket.

"Thanks;" he said and passed into the little parlor.

A man rose to meet him, tall, keen eyed, with blond hair and a scarred face. His age was probably about sixty, but he was upright and obviously fit.

"Good morning, Mr. Coward," he said softly, offering his hand. "Please sit down."

He said a few words in Polish to his wife, who returned to the shop, closing the door behind her. She would no doubt keep Fritz talking and allay any vague suspicions that his rather slow mind might be capable of forming. Coward almost regretted to see her go, and must have shown it in his face.

"You like my wife?" asked the man, smiling.

Coward diffidently agreed. "She is quite young?"

"Yes, very much younger than me. A good wife and a true Pole. Her good looks put you to the test, my friend. If you had tried any, shall we say, familiarities, we should have known that you were easily deflected from the task of defeating the Germans at Auschwitz, and left you very much alone."

Coward nodded, inwardly not a little put out that the lady's allure during his first visit had had such a mundane motive.

"However, Mr. Coward," continued the photographer, "I am pleased to say that our investigations of you have proved satisfactory. But may I say very clearly that if in future you should attempt to betray us in any way whatever, your life will not be worth that—" and he clicked his fingers. "I may assure you that our betrayers never escape us."

"Us? Who are you?"

"We are the Polish Underground Army and you will help in the greatest cause of the war by coming in with us and exterminating the filthy Germans in Auschwitz. My name is Otto. Just that, Otto. I am a member of the organization. We are very large. Our membership includes every Pole, no matter where he may be."

"I see," said Coward slowly. "I wondered what the hell was going on. What with the liaison between the optician and yourself, and the fact that I was being investigated, I knew some kind of organization was at work, but couldn't think what. The Polish Underground Army . . . and a damn fine idea, too." He thrust out his hand. "I'm with you a hundred per cent."

"Thank you. And now to business. There are several things we would like you to do for us, but first let me tell you a little about our work." Otto leaned back, clasping and unclasping his hands, an action symbolic of the restless patriotism within him. In his low voice and fastidious English he carried on. "You may not know it, but over half of the people who are gassed and destroyed in the Birkenau section of the Auschwitz camp are Gentiles. As a single race the Jews suffer, of course, the most, but every nation which the German attempts to crush—Poland, Czech, Greek, Bulgarian, Hungarian, French, Dutch and so on—yields its quota for Auschwitz. All are brought here to work and die. Some just to die. And the ovens and death pits ensure that about twenty-four thousand of them do so every twenty-four hours, a neat equation which appeals to the Germanic mind." He paused. "Concerned as we are about all those unhappy people, our main object is to help our own countrymen and to this end we have established a column of our Resistance actually among the prisoners in the camp. They are there all the time, working and watching for the opportunity to strike. In many ways they have already done good work, holding up the full production of buna. They do what they can to organize revolts among the wretches who are due for the gas chambers and many Germans have died as a result." He licked his thin lips, his face, on which the scars seemed to glow more lividly, set like a mask. "But to do these things, they must have outside contact—men who can go into the factory and pass over to them the tools for the job. The other sergeant major of the Britishers started this work and we had actually given him some arms when he was taken ill and had to return to Lamsdorf. We want you to carry on and get these things into the buna factory and Birkenau."

"I've got the guns you gave the other chap. Tell me who I'm to contact and I'll get it done right away."

Otto gave him instructions clearly, emphasizing his points with his clasped hands.

"We know you have men working inside the factory as well as outside, digging those trenches for the power lines. If you can get the guns past the guards at the gate you are to enter the main factory and go into the cellars. There you will be met by a man called Hecke. It is not his real name. He will know who you are and will take your guns, probably giving you a message for us. You will do this as often as you can. When you want supplies, contact me."

"Suppose something prevents you from coming to the camp to take the men's pictures, or I can't get down to see you here?"

"We shall always be able to reach you, Mr. Coward. Our people will never be far from you."

"Right. I'll start tomorrow. Is that all for now?"

"For now," agreed Otto, smiling suddenly. "And thank you."

Coward walked out into the shop, to find Fritz in conversation so deep with Mrs. Otto that his interest seemed decidedly more than fatherly.

"Come on, Fritzie," he called. "Time to be moving."

So began the most anxious and dangerous period of Coward's life.

Approaching the main gates of Auschwitz factory, he could feel his heart thumping. His duties as Red Cross delegate to the British element often took him through the buildings and camps to see men working there, and sometimes he penetrated into the administrative offices with complaints for the ears of the I.G. Farben managers. Not unknown at the gates, he had for some time been sweetening the various duty guards with presents of cigarettes and packets of coffee: all such bribes came from the Red Cross supplies of the British prisoners, an eloquent commentary on their confidence in Coward that they willingly donated part of their precious smokes and food in a cause of which they knew very little. It was so secret that none of Coward's friends were aware of the details; they trusted him to use the goods properly and their trust was never misplaced. So that he could be well furnished with cigarettes for bribery, he had stopped smoking himself, and several others followed suit, content to receive his word that their extra gifts of cigarettes were being put to good use.

He was let into the camp by two of the guards who knew him well. Name and number duly noted in a book, he walked on into the factory, painfully conscious of the pressure inside his battledress blouse. There, made up into paper parcels tied around his chest, were two automatics and several clips of ammunition, their weight making it an effort to square his shoulders. Luckily, during these excursions into the factory he invariably left his own guard at the gates, so being comparatively free to wander around by himself.

He stopped first by a party of some twenty British prisoners who were working manfully on the foundations of what were to be the dynamos for the electrical installations. Active though they were, very little real work was being done and the concrete poured from a mixer was splashed about with abandon. Coward had a few words with his boys, to the evident dissatisfaction of the onlooking guards, and then moved on to where another party was engaged on the far side of the factory. Around him worked the slave gangs, silently and with many a blow from their half-animal overseers. Although the beatings and brutality were daily occurrences, he could never accustom himself to watching them; his gorge still rose as he saw the treatment meted out to those poor scraps of humanity.

Slowly he made his way down one of the aisles and through a great bay in which machinery hummed. To one side here, he knew, were the cellars, infamous places where the deportee prisoners who had died on each day's shift were thrown until they were collected later by the *Sonderkommandos* for extinction in the furnaces. These *Sonderkommandos* were themselves deportees who had bargained for an extra few miserable weeks of life by becoming attendants at the gas chambers. It was their task to pull out the corpses after the gas had done its work on the luckless prisoners who had thought they were about to be shower-bathed, and so many bodies would claw over each other in their last death throes that specially spiked poles had been devised to drive into the flesh and haul them out. The *Sonderkommandos* would remove all hair from the bodies, a valuable war material, and all teeth, most especially the gold ones so beloved of Continental peoples, then pile the bodies on steel trucks that ran straight to the furnaces. Many of these gruesome attendants went mad or asked for death themselves; in any event, few survived the job for more than a few weeks. Some of them were compelled to pull the bodies of their own families from the chambers and load them into the fires. The horror of it all defies full comprehension.

Coward glanced casually around. None of the throngs of half-dead workers appeared to be watching, no German was actually in sight, and the *kapo* overseers were intent on their charges. He slipped through the door to the cellars and stumbled down dark steps.

As he reached the bottom, a hand gripped his arm, a voice said:

"Coward?"

He felt the roots of his hair tingle.

"Yes. Are you—?"

"Hecke. You have guns?"

In almost complete darkness, he handed over the paper parcels, hearing the man give an intake of breath as he felt their weight.

"Is good. Thank you."

His hand was seized and shaken with pathetically little grip. The man seemed to be trying to croak his gratitude in almost unintelligible English and Coward felt the back of his eyes suddenly sting with tears.

"All right, old son, don't bother," he said quickly. "I'll bring more, as soon as I can. What about tomorrow?"

"Sprechen Sie langsam. Ich verstehe nicht."

"Tomorrow—*morgen. Um wieviel Uhr?"*

"No, no. Seven days, yes?"

"Okay. In a week, then." He pressed a bar of chocolate into the man's hand and knew by the way the
shadowy figure stiffened that it was in the last stages
of starvation. He patted the man on the shoulder,
hearing, as he climbed the steps again, sounds of the
chocolate being ravenously consumed. Half an hour
later, having arrived by circuitous route at the main
gate, he discovered himself to be bathed in sweat and
trembling violently.

In a week's time, skillfully avoiding the questions of
Clatterbridge, he gathered together the remaining
guns and the hand grenades from under the floor
boards and in the privacy of his little cubicle once more
strung them around his chest. At the guardhouse Fritz
waited to take up his faithfully plodding station behind
him, but he was astonished to find the German in a
resplendent new uniform.

"Blimey, Fritz, they made you a field marshal or
something?" The German grinned. "Phew! Quite a get-
up, isn't it? Big improvement, I must say. Is there a
big shot coming today?"

"Zis wear when I go mit Count, always. Orders,
Kommandant orders, so."

"Count? What Count? Are you leaving me?"

The guard grinned more broadly than ever.

"Well, hang this for a lark!" exclaimed Coward angrily, incensed at the thought of the time and gifts he
had wasted on bringing Fritz to the right "attitude." He
stamped into the guardhouse and practically launched
himself at the desk of the *Unteroffizier* inside. "I want
to register an official complaint. I want you to trans-
mit it immediately to your superior officer, and I will
send a copy of it to the Protecting Power in Switzerland."

The *Unteroffizier* jumped to his feet, worried.

"Entschuldigen Sie bitte," he stammered and hurried
into the inner office, re-appearing with the duty officer.

"Look here," Coward shouted, before that worthy could open his mouth. "I represent the Red Cross and I've got a job of work to do in this camp. Do you agree or don't you?" The officer nodded, growing a little red at the onslaught. "The authorities will take a serious view of you trying to impede essential Red Cross work, I can tell you."

"But—"

"I've had old Fritz for some time now." Coward gestured wildly at the open doorway. "I've mothered that ape, taught him English, got him familiar with my routine. I'm damned if I'm going to start all over again with someone else."

"Sergeant major—"

"Today I came to collect him for my rounds and without any warning at all find him dressed up like a dog's dinner so he can wet nurse some bloody aristocrat. What is this place, the flipping savoy? This is deliberate obstruction of Red Cross work and I demand to see—"

"Silence!" roared the officer. He rapped out an order; the figure of Fritz appeared nervously in the doorway and saluted. There was a rapid exchange in German, then the officer, followed by the *Unteroffizier*, and lastly by Fritz himself, burst into laughter.

"If it's a joking matter—" began Coward, turning away angrily; as he moved there was an ominous clink beneath his blouse. For a second the eyes of the officer narrowed; then he stepped forward quickly.

"A moment," he said pleasantly. "What is your name?"

"My name?"

"*Wie heissen Sie?* What is your name?"

Coward breathed heavily. "Take me to the *Kommandant*," he said quietly. "Take me before we all go mad. If you don't know my name by now—"

"Ah, we know you by one name, Mr. Coward. Now there is another also."

"What d'you mean? Am I Napoleon Bonaparte as well?"

"Not quite, my friend. But you are, so I am told, the Count of Auschwitz."

Coward stared. "The Count of Auschwitz? I don't know what the hell you're talking about."

"Permit me to enlighten you. Your personal smartness and bearing has aroused comment for some time, earning you the title of the Count among some of our soldiers. This has reached the ears of the *Kommandant*, who has himself noticed how disreputable your guard looked in comparison when you are both outside the camp. The *Kommandant* is very displeased and has ordered that any guard accompanying you will wear a new uniform. Your—er—Fritz has therefore drawn his new outfit and we have no intention—at the moment—of depriving you of his services."

Coward threw back his head and laughed.

"I'm sorry I blew up," he said, after a minute. "I'm glad, though, that things are going to be smartened up. Well, I must be off to work."

Fritz followed him out. "Ze Count is ready?" he asked with portentous gravity.

"Yes, whistle up the carriage," grinned Coward. "And button your collar, you big cheese."

Inside the factory, he waited his chance, then again slipped down to the cellar, passing Hecke some bread and meat in addition to the arms. This time he was aware of a number of corpses sprawled near them on the damp stone floor. Hecke merely pointed to them and said, "Die today."

While in the factory he paid a visit to the "Personnel Manager" of I.G. Farben to complain of the food given to his working parties. The official, a sleek, well-fed German from the upper classes, shrugged his shoulders.

"We do our best, Mr. Coward," he protested, "but conditions are bad. Food is hard to get. I will see what I can do, but cannot promise."

Coward glared at him truculently, seeing in him the cause of all the suffering in that foul place, blaming him personally for all the atrocities of the Germans.

"Try to make it better, *Herr Direktor,*" he snapped. "I shall put in a full report to the Red Cross authorities about the bad food here, and about other things too."

The plump German smiled bleakly, tapping his fingers on the desk. "What other things, Mr. Coward?"

"The beastly killings that go on by the thousand here every day, the Jews and other people gassed and burnt, the slaves beaten to death, and God knows what else!"

"God knows, perhaps, but I don't. Gassings? Killings? You must be out of your mind. Don't talk lightly of such things, Mr. Coward. It might be dangerous for you to make such wild statements about the government and this company."

Coward choked back the angry words that rose to his lips. Already he had said too much. He must go easy.

"All right, sir. You don't know anything about them. You probably wear dark spectacles when you walk around your factory."

The manager chuckled. "Exactly. I wear dark spectacles. May I advise you to do the same, Mr. Coward?"

Coward strode out, raging inwardly against this fat German, against the ghastly factory, against himself. His tongue ran away with him too easily. For other people's sake beside his own, he must be on his guard and keep a still tongue in his head.

That evening Otto the photographer arrived at the camp and, accompanied by an *Unteroffizier,* took pictures of the men in groups.

"I shall only be able to get through half the work tonight," he announced to Coward. "But next week I shall come more." His English had noticeably deteriorated, probably to impress the *Unteroffizier,* but when they were left alone for a moment he took this opportunity to whisper quickly, "Go to the optician's for more polishing rags." Here we go again, thought Coward.

In a couple of days he returned to Berkenwald, ostensibly for another eye test and to take Clatterbridge's spectacles for adjustment. This time he really was accompanied by a new guard, Fritz having left on a short leave, so he padded out his blouse with paper, hoping that when he came back with the guns any added size would not attract interest. It was a dangerous game, but by now his original fears were beginning to evaporate and he had in their place a strange exultation, a keen excitement such as a hunter feels in the chase. He was met as before by Jan, who carried out the necessary examination of his eyes and slipped four pistols into his blouse while so doing, literally under the nose of the German soldier. To keep him occupied Jan had given the man a book of nude photographs; it did its job so well that Coward had almost to tear him away in order to catch the bus.

By the time this little load had been safely smuggled into the factory and delivered to Hecke in the cellars, Coward had begun to wonder when the show down would come, and it was nearer than he imagined.

One question in his mind was answered when Otto came to complete the taking of the photographs. The Pole contrived to steal a few minutes alone with Coward in his tiny cubicle office and immediately drew several little bundles from out of his professional case.

"Hide these. Get them to Hecke as soon as possible," he said urgently, then seeing Coward's puzzlement, hurried on, "Be careful how you handle them. They're sticks of dynamite from the German army stores at Breslau."

Removing the section of floorboard and gingerly placing the bundles underneath, Coward thought rapidly. "Just what the doctor ordered," he said cheerfully, "but how the blazes can I get them into the factory? They're too big to hide under my uniform."

Otto smiled. "I leave that to the British Army to solve, Mr. Coward. I have great faith in them, you know. All Polish people have."

"Well, we'll find a way, I suppose."

The photographer looked at him in silence for a moment. "You know, sergeant major," he said then very quietly, "we Poles have long memories, not only for hurts done to us, but for favors too. We won't forget you, if we all get out of this alive."

He closed his case with a bang and walked slowly out of the hut, leaving Coward, still on his hands and knees in the corner, looking after him.

15

GUNRUNNING

A prized possession of the British prisoners was a small hand cart, consisting of one long handle running the entire length of the cart, with boards sloping outward from the shaft to form a V-shaped body. With this useful carrier, Coward and an assistant would pick up the mail from the railway station at Auschwitz and distribute it to the various small working parties in and around the factory, delivering letters and carrying parcels back to the barracks for collection when the men returned at night. So it happened that one day, when he and his diminutive partner in this task, Tich Keenan, pushed the cart as usual to the station, there already reposed under its empty sacks a parcel addressed to Coward and containing dynamite.

They trailed back to the factory and drew up at the gates, waiting for admission. Their names were noted, the cart given a cursory inspection, and they were waved on their way. Already Coward was becoming known to many of the slaves who knew that he was often able to slip them some morsel of food as he passed, daring the wrath of the *kapo* to do so. They would risk a beating to swallow a crust of bread and often tried to crowd near him so that he might see them. This happened as the Britishers trundled their cart across the yard to the main building. Always deeply touched by these hungry human animals, Coward guided the cart so that it would pass near a group of the wretches in their striped pyjama tunics.

Tich eyed them commiseratingly. "Poor devils," he

muttered. "Makes your bloody heart bleed, don't it?"

Coward passed one fellow a potato. The man was immediately smashed over the back by the *kapo's* cudgel and the Britishers were subjected to a stream of invective, which they returned with interest. The cart creaked on into the factory itself and continued its course until they had reached the entrance to the cellars. Then Coward stopped.

"Have a look at the wheels, Tich," he said. "I'm sure you can find something wrong."

He gathered up the parcels of dynamite and made his way down into the cellars. The only people present were those who had no further interest in this world, but Coward slipped the parcel into a crevice prearranged with Hecke, and rejoined Keenan just as an *Unteroffizier* arrived on the scene with a gang of deportees. Before them they pushed a handcart heaped with dead, at least nine bodies. The toll had been heavy on the last shift. The German stood waiting while the slaves heaved the corpses one by one down the cellar steps, where Coward had so lately been. It was a close call and he longed to mop his face.

The *Unteroffizier,* bluff and red-faced, seemed disposed to talk, and turned to the Britisher who seconds before had planted a substantial charge of high explosive beneath his very feet.

"Plenty dies last night, eh?" he said in a cheery tone which a bank manager might employ to discuss his golf.

Coward agreed, humoring his mood in case he might learn something.

The German went on with heavy facetiousness, "Want to buy any, eh? Going cheap."

A thought leaped into Coward's mind. If only the man were serious.

"How much would you want for them, *Herr Unteroffizier?* I could use a few sometimes."

The man's face was a study. The humor of it had got beyond him. He drew nearer.

"You want to buy bodies? What for?"

"Never you mind what for," answered Coward affably, fighting down his disgust. "I can pay you coffee, cigarettes, soap, chocolate." An idea, grotesque yet perhaps just possible, was forming.

The German looked warily about, then said, "Say when and you can have as many as you like."

"I want, say, three this day next week. Right? I want them dumped in the ditch between the factory and Birkenau. *Verstehen Sie?*"

Frightened and puzzled as he was, the German succumbed to his greed for such magical things as coffee and chocolate. "Right, *Herr Feldwebel*. I see you here tomorrow—you pay me then."

The Britishers moved on. As soon as they were out of earshot, Tich exclaimed:

"Stone the crows, Charlie, what's the game? What d'you want to buy three stiff'uns for?"

"This is the idea, Tich. You know that every night a bunch of these poor bastards who are not fit to work any more are marched across to Birkenau to be gassed? Right. If I can arrange with them beforehand to get three of them to drop off the column in the dark and then shoot the dead 'uns in to the road, they'll have a chance to escape. We'll have to get some kit for them to wear, but after that it'll be up to them. At least they'll have a sporting chance, and that's more than they'll get inside Birkenau."

Keenan looked at him admiringly.

"You're a perishing genius, Charlie—even if you are as cracked as an old chamber pot."

"Never mind the compliments, Tich. We've got to work fast. We can tell the Jews that we'll help some of them to escape if they will do a spot of sabotage in the factory, so we'll be killing two birds with one stone."

Then began one of the strangest escape stories of all time; one of the most macabre, at all events. That afternoon, by dint of joining them in the lee of the building as they drank their meager supply of watery *kraut* soup, Coward got into touch with a group of Jews: gaunt, ragged creatures, their bodies shrunken or distended with malnutrition, hands and faces covered with sores. One tall man who came from Hungary and had been a lawyer before the *SS* snatched him up, spoke English well and offered to act as liaison officer for Coward. He was to keep an eye on those picked for the furnaces and warn three of them the following week to watch out for Coward and Tich on the road to the extermination camp. In return he pledged himself and his friends to do as much damage in the factory as their puny strength was capable of, although to observe a certain discretion so that wholesale slaughter would not result as a reprisal. He was as good as his word and many times did those living corpses break a wire or wreck a machine, some of them unhappily dying in the attempt. Coward even heard from the lawyer of one young Jew who had thrown himself onto a whirring dynamo, knowing that his body would effectively jam it for some time. This knowledge, the thought that he was driving some of these gallant people to their death weeks or months before they would have died at the hands of the Hun, saddened him, yet such deaths were blows for freedom, raising morale tremendously, and better than tame submission to die when it suited the overlords.

Meantime, he and Tich were indefatigable in their efforts to obtain some kind of civilian clothing; by spending much of the men's cigarettes and soap (they had been let into this particular secret and highly approved of it) enough miscellaneous articles were acquired for three people. On the day following the conversation with the *Unteroffizier,* Coward had met him as arranged and paid over two bars of chocolate and twenty cigarettes. He said in English as the bargain closed:

"You know, you horrible swine you, the last time a Jew cost thirty pieces of silver. I'm getting them at cut price, aren't I? About a shilling each!"

He turned away, feeling sick, knowing that the German would not let him down for fear of Coward disclosing the deal to the authorities.

As darkness fell on the fateful evening, he and Tich Keenan approached the guard on the gate of their own camp. What they were about to do was not particularly unusual; it only happened on working parties, but it did happen. The guard winked at them.

"Going out?" he asked.

Coward leered back. "Just for an hour. Must look after our girls, you know." He slipped the inevitable bribe into the man's waiting hand and they passed through. Escape this way would be easy, he thought. And sighed as he realized the impossibility of attempting it in his present position. They hurried down the road, keeping well in to the hedge. The guard watched them go, envying them their apparent trip to the local brothel.

Soon they came to the small road that led from Auschwitz proper to Birkenau, whose chimneys cast a

lurid red glow over the night sky. All five furnaces were working hard and both men felt a sense of unreality in the scene. It seemed unbelievable that those fires could really be consuming human beings by the dozen every minute, that the hair of the victims really was saved for cushions and pillows, that the daily cartloads of barrels of fat were the last remains of a great multitude of people whose final destiny was to provide perhaps an ingredient for bars of soap. Yet in the ditch lay the answer to such doubts: three rigid bodies, sightless eyes upturned to the sky, hands clenched.

"Here they are," whispered Tich, shuddering involuntarily as he looked down at them. They crouched near the corpses, doing their best to control their stomachs.

It was a cold, eerie wait of one and a half hours before a long string of apathetic creatures came winding up the road, their faces dimly discernible in the glow from the furnaces toward which they were heading. All feeling seemed knocked out of them. At their head walked three guards; behind the column of about two hundred slaves walked three more. The Germans were not taking too much notice. They knew only too well that if any of the doomed people were missing when they were counted at the gates at Birkenau, it would be an easy job to round them up, dressed as they were and in that pitiable condition. The victims were always told that they were being taken for a shower bath and many of the wretches believed this until the last dreadful moment when the great doors of the baths clanged shut and faces, lifted up to receive the benison of water from the sprays, received instead hydrate of cyanide from a vent in the hollow pillars.

The Britishers crouched low in the ditch as the column wound past. According to the instructions Coward had given the lawyer, the three chosen to make the attempt should be in the middle of the column and would drop into the ditch about here. Breathlessly he watched to see if they would have the nerve: if they funked it at the last moment and three bodies were

found in the next day without a compensating three
missing from the Birkenau count, there would be the
devil to pay. Then he hissed sharply between his teeth.
He saw three shadowy figures detach themselves from
the main body and slither into the ditch not twenty
yards from where he and Tich lay. Down he bobbed
and waited until all the column had straggled by and
the three Germans at the rear had passed, chattering
noisily and laughing. As the tail of the column disappeared, he and Tich dragged up the corpses and laid
them at well spaced intervals by the side of the road,
as if they had fallen and not been noticed. It often
did happen that men and women died on their way to
Birkenau; when they were counted at the gates and
found to be so many short, a man was always dis-
patched back along the road to find the bodies. If the
tally agreed, then all was well and no further action
taken.

Hurriedly they pulled the civilian clothing from beneath their battledress and scrambled along to where
the three deportees crouched shivering in the wet ditch.
They looked up as the two Britishers approached.

"Put these on," said Coward urgently, "and run—
run like hell. Go to the back of the photographer's in
Auschwitz. Don't be seen. He'll help you."

They could scarcely understand him, but the necessity for speed gripped them all with a deadly terror.
Without a word they wrenched on the clothes, their
movements peculiarly jerky and mechanical. Coward
repeated his instructions, though with little hope that
they meant anything at all, then faced the men in the
right direction and pushed them gently on their way.
One of them caught his sleeve in a mute gesture of
gratitude, then they were off, stumbling in the darkness.

"Good luck, lads," said Coward, half to himself.

Back at the camp, the two friends told the story to
their fellows and an immediate whip around was the
answer for some more goods with which to buy bodies.
Something had certainly started.

On his journeys through the factory and surrounding camps Coward was now accorded a new respect, for although only a few of the Jews were in the secret of the escape system, word had got around that he was helping deportees in some way. His new name, too, quickly spread by unknown channels, and a Frenchman surprised him considerably one day by addressing him, with a flourish, as "M. le Comte," a strange appellation which pleased his French comrades immensely. To this day Coward is called "The Count" by people whom he scarcely knows; among the hundreds who did manage to evade the lash of German fury at Auschwitz in its latter days, hardly a person failed to recognize the man with the honorary title. And truly he lived up to the name, for he ruled the roost there more effectively than did many of the German officers.

Then came the occasion when, delivering to Hecke some pistols which he continued to procure from either Otto or Jan, he heard the gaunt man ask hoarsely for more dynamite.

"You want more? What do you do with it? Eat it?"

If Hecke understood the joke, he gave no reaction.

"I go, soon, *Herr* Coward. More dynamite first."

"Go? Where are you going?"

"Birkenau."

Coward stood still in the darkness, shocked. He had grown to like this brave man whom he met only infrequently in the grim morgue of the cellars.

"Are you sure?" he asked, his throat dry.

"Next week. It is sure. More dynamite first."

"But—good God, man let's get you out. I won't let them take you—"

"No. My work nearly done. They will not take me. I take them. With dynamite."

"But I won't be seeing Otto for several days—"

Coward felt the touch of bony fingers on his arm.

"Please. You must try. I have little time."

"Leave it to me, Hecke. I'll do what I can. Meet me here tomorrow."

He came out of the factory deeply worried. It meant a night trip to the photographer's shop, something he had never attempted before. Besides that, on the following evening he had another consignment of Jews expected from the corpse dealer. This time there had been six to pay for, and there would be six live members of the death column to extricate from their hell. It was all beginning to crowd in on him.

It was now early summer and dusk did not fall until very late. Just before eleven thirty he left his hut, knowing that it was too late to get through the gates by bribery. The guards were always amenable to this form of coercion but they insisted on absentees being back by ten in good time for the duty officer's rounds at eleven. There was no help for it. He had to go through the wire. That evening a group of his pals had sat playing cards against the two wires surrounding the camp and during the game Coward had got to work with a pair of pliers and made a small hole through which he could just crawl. He crept out now, wriggling his way across the ground, taking advantage of every scrap of cover. Then, timing the sweeping searchlights to a second, he shot forward and struggled through the hole, hugging the ground again on the other side as the powerful beam returned. Soon he was running as hard as he could in the direction of Auschwitz, taking short cuts which he had memorized for just such an emergency as this. Within half an hour he was pressed, painfully breathless, against the fence of the back garden to Otto's house, the rough boards cooling his hot cheek. There was complete silence. He waited until he breathed normally, then scaled the fence and dropped into the darkness of the garden. He walked without a sound to the back door and tapped on it softly. Nothing happened. He tapped again, louder, and waited.

Suddenly it opened. Still there was no light, but Coward made out the figure of Otto in a dressing gown, a revolver in his hand. He saw the Pole relax as he was recognized.

"Come in." The door closed quietly behind them. "Mr. Coward, what are you doing here? This is dangerous."

"It's Hecke," explained Coward as he was led into a small room where Otto switched on a dim light. "He says he's due for Birkenau next week. He must have some more dynamite first."

Otto slipped the gun into his pocket.

"I have expected this," he said thoughtfully. "Hecke knew that his end would be soon; he only asked that when it came, the means of his going would be in his own hands. We cannot fail him now."

He left the room, motioning Coward to pour himself a glass of *schnapps,* and almost immediately his wife entered looking very becoming in her dressing gown and flushed with sleep.

"An unexpected pleasure, Mr. Coward," she said with a smile. "You have taken a big risk coming here."

"Hecke takes a bigger one, madam."

They sat down facing each other, and Coward found himself regarding her with appreciation.

"I am thankful you are not a Frenchman, Mr. Coward," she said very softly. "I have heard that they are swift to act when left alone with a woman." Coward grinned feebly and sipped his drink. "Never mind," she went on, "let us hope that soon you will be home in England again with lots of nice girls to take out."

"Lady, spare me blushes. I'm a married man with a family. Have a heart!"

Rather awkwardly, they both laughed, then fell silent. Presently the silence became oppressive. Coward stretched over to a small table and gently set down his empty glass. At that instant a heavy blow resounded on the front door of the shop and a voice roared:

"Raus, Schweinehund! Open!"

He saw the girl's face go white and leapt for the back door, colliding with Otto in the passageway.

"Gestapo!" gasped the photographer. "Quick—out at the back, if you can. We'll try to cover up."

Coward received the package thrust into his hands, but as he moved there came the explosion of a bullet fired into the lock on the front door, followed a moment later by the sound of heavy feet tramping into the shop. He tightened his grip on the package, such an innocent package containing about ten pounds of dynamite; he took a deep breath, then plunged forward.

16

DYNAMITE INTO THE FURNACES

"Otto!" He heard the girl's scream above the confusion of voices and learned only afterward that she had simulated a very real terror that their house had been broken into by drunkards or brigands or both. Her shrieks of protests and shouts for the police drowned even the angry orders of the *Gestapo* as he raced for the back door, slammed it behind him and stumbled down the garden, hugging to himself his fragile load. It was a tricky task to heave himself over the fence with one hand and required all his strength. At one time, so agonizingly slow did it seem before he found purchase on the top of the fence, all was surely lost—the back door was certainly about to burst open and spill out furious Germans into the garden. Then he was down on the other side, revelling for a fleeting instant in the curious fact that the back of the house had not been covered, and running, as fast as he could with reasonable safety, into the darkness.

Over the fields and hedges he scrambled on until he judged he was safe, then stopping to recover his breath and take stock of his position. He thought grimly of the fate that Otto and his wife would almost certainly suffer at the hands of the *Gestapo;* the girl's uproar had enabled him to get away, but it could scarcely achieve more. They were two exceedingly brave and gallant people whom he knew he would never see again. With a heavy heart he resumed his journey, more stealthily now as he neared the camp. The butterflies in his stomach had quietened a little, but the hand holding the package of dynamite trembled as he realized the job of breaking in that now lay before him.

Yet in the event it was not so difficult, at least for someone as expert in timing the swinging searchlight beams as he had become. A very slight mist had risen from the marshy ground; under its wispy but valuable cloak he soon located the clipped wires, waited till the exactly right moment, wriggled through still gripping the explosive, and tore into the comforting shadows of his barracks. Once inside, a wave of reaction turned his knees to jelly. He lowered the package carefully into the space beneath the floorboards, reached for his bunk, and flopped on to it.

Tich and Coward made their usual trip for mail the next morning. Coward dared not call in so early at the photographer's shop, but stole a glance at it as they made a detour to pass it by. All was silent and closed up; outside lounged an obvious *Gestapo* man, immaculate in his black uniform, and he looked hard at the trio of two prisoners and Fritz as they trundled the cart past him. He said nothing, but spat expressively into the gutter, watching them as they carried on up the street.

"Nice geezer, that," commented Tich. "Couldn't look happier if he'd just bumped off his grandmother."

"He probably has," said Coward wondering if the man had been one of the party in the shop the previous night.

They collected the parcels and letters, packing them gently around the package of dynamite. Tich had no idea how Coward had come by it, and knew better than to ask, but he needed no second warning to treat it with care. They made their way back leisurely to the factory, and if Fritz noticed the anxiety with which they avoided pot holes, he was too well trained to make any remark. The usual preliminaries completed at the gate, they began their rounds of the working parties. Coward waited some time for an opportunity to visit the cellars; eventually the coast was clear and he descended the steps to the rank-smelling dungeon. Hecke was already there, his quick shallow breathing clearly audible in the darkness.

"Bitte—Haben Sie?" asked the Pole without a word of greeting.

"Yes. It's had a bit of rough passage getting here."

"Ah!" A hand travelled down Coward's arm until it reached the package. *"Danke schön. . . Auf Wiedersehen."*

"What d'you mean—goodbye?"

"Morgen. I go."

"Wo?" Breathed the Britisher excitedly.

"Birkenau."

Coward was thunderstruck. "Hecke," he whispered urgently, "listen to me. Let me arrange an escape like the others. You understand? It'll give you a chance—"

"No, no. You good man." A paroxysm of muffled coughing racked the other man. "Lungs—*kaput. Morgen*—I go—Birkenau."

"Um wieviel Uhr?"

"Früh, Auf Wie—"

"Es tut mir leid."

"Es macht nichts." Coward felt himself gently pushed. *"Geh' fort! Danke!"*

He rejoined Tich, and they walked on, out into the bright sunlight. Another gone, then, of the brave and resolute band who fought without personal hope against such overwhelming odds. He thought of Corporal Reynolds, whose ready support of the clandestine operations at Auschwitz had come to such sudden and tragic end on the pylon detail; of Otto and his wife, who, if they were not dead already, could not have long to live; and again he swore a retribution. His heart felt leaden as he wheeled the cart along, and he sought to ease the pain inside him a little by fishing scraps of food from his pockets and passing them to some of the deportees. Many of the slaves had come to know him well, for whispers were already circulating of the part he played in rescuing some of the condemned during their last walk to the gas chambers. The oncoming light evenings had added a further complication, making an even greater degree of care absolutely vital, for one false move would have brought terrible punishment, not only upon the heads of the Britishers but the entire Jewish camp. But now the "Count of Auschwitz" had paid over considerable fees in the form of chocolates and cigarettes to the *Unteroffizier* in charge of the bodies; only the day before that worthy had offered a whole lorryload for two hundred smokes. What he imagined Coward's business was with the corpses no one will ever know, but he must have been singularly guileless if he failed to guess the truth.

Then, later the same day, Fritz unwittingly brought wonderful news. The raid on Otto's shop was the topic of conversation amongst all the guards and, so the story went, had proved amazingly abortive. Two *Gestapo* agents had chanced to pass the shop on their way back from the local *Gasthaus* and spotting a gleam of light from the oil lamp, had immediately suspected that only something illegal could be going on so late at night. Suspicion being always sufficient justification for throwing their weight about, they had broken in. Things would have gone hard with them if they had indeed surprised a group of ruthless Resistance men at work. As it was, Otto's wife had rushed full tilt into them when they were barely inside and her commotion had delayed their half-drunken progress long enough for Coward to make good his escape. A long session of questioning had followed at the police station as a matter of course, but after several hours Otto was released and his wife retained in custody. This was a tremendous relief to Coward, but he was worried for the woman. He knew what dreadful forms a *Gestapo* interrogation could take and feared for her life, especially as she was Polish and therefore anathema to the Germans.

Only much later did he hear the rest of the story, fortunately a fairly happy ending. For two days the *Gestapo* had continued their questioning, keeping the girl without sleep or food until she repeatedly fainted. But she had held on wonderfully, not saying a word about her husband's Underground activities. Eventually freed, she had staggered home in a pitiful condition but at least alive. Her shoulders and breasts were burnt with cigarette ends, her mouth swollen, her fingernails broken and bleeding where sharp splinters had been forced down them. But her spirits were completely undaunted. The Germans had not shaken her story that she and her husband had been trying to alleviate his toothache. That explained the glasses of *schnapps* and, thank heaven, Otto did have a tooth that was obviously decayed. It was a slender story, yet due to the absence of any incriminating evidence in the house it had held and the courageous couple are probably alive to this day.

The next two days were enlivened by an air raid alarm. This was the first time that the American air force had paid their respects so close to Auschwitz and a rumble of bombs could be heard from a neighboring town. After the raid two Fortresses, their sight gladdening the heart of every prisoner, circled over the great sprawling mass of camps and dropped leaflets. Coward got hold of one of the circling scraps of paper and read with interest an announcement that Auschwitz was next on the list for annihilation and a warning that all non-combatants should move to a safer zone. The leaflets brought wry smiles to the faces of the prisoners. The Allies were still playing at their gentlemen's war; their concern for the safety of the forced workers compelled them to advertise their intentions in advance, thereby giving the enemy plenty of time in which to move up fighter wings and organize anti-aircraft defenses.

Although Coward did not realize it at the time, the information about Auschwitz which he was sending back in the carefully contrived letters addressed to "William Orange," and which were duly finding their way to the Intelligence branch of the War Office, was of direct help in the framing of leaflets calling upon the German population to rise against such atrocities, and one or two conspicuous broadcasts on the same subject by distinguished British war leaders.

It was in the evening of the second day after his

narrow escape at the photographer's shop that the miraculous, the dreamed-of, happened.

He was sitting at the table in his little office with Tich Keenan and several of the other men, playing cards and sipping tea, when a tremendous explosion seized the ground with both hands and shook it violently.

"Holy smoke, he's done it!" bawled Coward as they scrambled outside, white-faced and trembling in spite of themselves.

At the wire stood Clatterbridge, waving his arms and shouting, "Witness! Thus shall fall the ungodly!" They followed the direction of his pointing arm. In the distance over Birkenau a pall of black smoke rose slowly in the evening sky. They watched it fascinatedly and to their ears came the far-away sounds of pistol shots. In a few moments two cars packed with soldiers roared past, driving furiously to the scene of the explosion. All the prisoners were out of their barracks, and now that the initial shock was over had begun to conjecture wildly on what had happened.

"Good man. Oh, good man," breathed Coward to himself. Hecke had died by his own hand after all, but no doubt taking a good many of his captors with him.

"They've blown up the furnaces!" jabbered Tich excitedly. "That's what they've done—blows the swine up!"

"By God, I think you're right," exclaimed Coward.

Scarcely had he spoken when another terrible concussion ripped through the evening air, this time much nearer. Several of the men dived to the ground, fearful that they were being bombed, but Coward and Tich knew better. They watched as a gout of debris shot up from the nearby factory and spumed lazily out.

"Just look at that!" muttered Tich in awe.

"There go some men with real guts," said Coward quietly. He stood for a few seconds without speaking. After the ear-splitting detonations, the silence seemed heavy and the ejaculations of the prisoners were low in tone. Then, "Did you get that timing, Tich?" he asked more briskly. "First they let the furnaces at Bir-

kenau have it, to distract attention from the factory; then they upped something in the factory itself. A beautiful job."

"What a crowd!"

"Yes, they're some crowd all right—God rest 'em. This'll give Jerry a few sore places to lick for a while. Don't know about you, Tich, but I could use a good strong cup of tea. Pity we haven't any *schnapps* to celebrate with. Tonight calls for something better than char."

The next day saw the full extent of the damage. In the factory Coward's men were given the job of clearing up after the second explosion. It seemed that the charge had been laid beneath the great new generators that had been placed in position only the previous week on the base built for them by the Britishers. Now the site presented a picture of gutted machinery and twisted steel. It began to look as if the factory would

never get into full production. In point of fact it never did.

In due course the Britishers were able to piece together the story of that evening. Hecke and a group of his inmates were part of the death gang marched along the road to Birkenau, and as there had been a lull in the steady stream to the gas chambers the column had been ordered straight down the ramp and in to the "showers." Hecke had immediately blown open the far door with a hand grenade and led his men along the miniature railway track to the crematorium, firing their guns into the faces of the startled guards. Four of them survived to reach the furnaces. It was an easy matter to toss the dynamite into the glowing red maw, and then it was all over. Three of the five furnaces had been put out of action and about thirty guards slaughtered.

Coward's work had not been for nothing. His risks

had paid dividends and he was well content, except for the thought of those men who had died for their cause. True, they had been doomed anyway, but their loss was none the less cruel.

From that time on the Germans tightened their security measures to an extent that made further smuggling impossible. All the deportees entering and leaving both the buna factory and Birkenau were searched minutely and it became the practice for slaves entering the extermination camp to strip completely naked so that no arms could possibly be concealed. The road leading from one camp to the other came under close watch, as it was there the Germans suspected that pistols had been passed to the prisoners, and escapes by means of substituted bodies had to cease. Still, by this time the ruse had served its purpose for nearly four hundred men.

Coward chafed restlessly at the sudden inactivity and sought fresh pastures. Visits to the many camps in the Auschwitz-Monowitz-Sossnowitz area convinced him that the accommodation available left no excuse for the pitiful overcrowding of the deportees; he demanded an interview with the Farben administrators, demanded it afresh when no response appeared to be forthcoming, and eventually was summoned to the canteen in the German staff block. He found himself facing several Farben officials and SS officers who were seated at a long table. An interpreter was present and he asked Coward to proceed.

"The most important thing that concerns me," said Coward, "is this. Is it true that thousands of civilian prisoners are being gassed and cremated?"

There was silence for a moment, then a Farben official laughed. Immediately all at the table were chuckling good-naturedly.

"Utter nonsense," said the man who had laughed, through the interpreter. "A crematorium is necessary to serve such a large area as this, in which many prisoners fall sick and die. It is hygenic, you must understand."

"What about the gassing of people who are alive?"

"Fairy tales. Where a great number of workers are

gathered together, one must expect the wildest rumors."

You swine, thought Coward; you only agreed to see me because you know I put in official complaints to the Red Cross. That isn't too healthy for you, although they can do nothing for the slaves. Now you'll admit nothing because of those *SS* brutes at your elbow. "You mentioned prisoners who fall sick," he said, not daring to make a direct accusation, and fighting down his anger. "Everywhere, including the Polish camps and the camp for Russian girls—even in the brothel for those who can go there—you display notices saying that sick personnel will be 'transferred.' What does this mean?"

"Naturally, that they will be removed to hospital or camps for lighter work."

"Do you know that the notices are interpreted as a threat—that sick people who are 'transferred' are believed to be taken to Birkenau and are not heard of again?"

"We have told you we cannot accept responsibility for stupid tales, Mr. Coward. Do not waste our time."

"I am disturbed by shooting which I often hear at night."

"You are mistaken. One worker did attempt to leave camp against orders recently. That is all."

"But surely, with all the guards and dogs you have, that would be suicide?"

"Nevertheless, an attempt was made."

"The civilians look terribly weak. Will you give permission for the British prisoners to pass any food they can't eat, such as tinned fish, to the Polish and other camps?"

The Farben official glanced at his colleagues, then answered, "That is not possible. The nutrition of the workers is adequate, but in any case it is not under our control."

It was useless. He put further questions, receiving similarly evasive replies, and left the meeting boiling inwardly. The position was one of frustration: in public the *SS* showed every deference to the Farben administrators, opening car doors for them and generally paying court, yet it was clear that the factory directors were frightened men.

One day Otto appeared in the British camp again, bringing glad news. He said that several of the Jews whom Coward had helped to escape had managed to reach freedom. A great number of those who had slipped away from the death march had been caught and many shot, while others had not been heard of, but the fact that some, however few, had succeeded, was an occasion for warm thanks.

"My comrades and I would like you to accept a small token of our gratitude," said Otto, taking a small parcel from his photographer's bag.

Coward looked quickly toward the door of his office in case a German was about, but all seemed quiet. He picked up the parcel, a curiously heavy one for its small size.

"What is it?" he asked.

Otto chuckled. "A present from the Underground given with the good wishes of us all, especially my wife. Look at it."

Coward unwrapped the paper carefully. In the palm of his hand lay an ingot of pure gold about the size of a matchbox.

"My God!" he exclaimed. "Where did this come from?"

Otto locked his bag again and sat on the edge of the table. "Our men in Birkenau steal it from the warehouse there. You should see that warehouse. For some reason it's called 'Canada' and it is an astonishing sight. In it are stored clothes, jewelry, watches— yes, even perambulators, belonging to the families brought to Auschwitz from all over Europe. You see, they are told by the Germans that they are coming to a good working camp and to be prepared to make a life of it. They bring everything they can carry in the way of valuables and essentials, and when they arrive—poof!—all their possessions are taken from them. When their turn comes for extermination, their gold teeth, if they have any, are extracted for melting down. With the ingots we are able to smuggle out, we

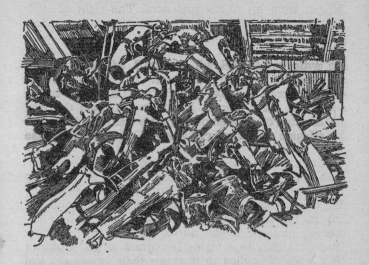

buy our guns and explosives, bribing the guards in armories elsewhere in the Reich. That gold, my friend, came from the teeth of murdered people."

Coward placed it hastily on the table, but Otto put out a restraining hand.

"No, don't be afraid to accept it. Do you think that the poor souls who provided it would not rather you had it than their murderers? You have earned it."

Coward picked up the ingot again, weighing it thoughtfully. The thought of using it to spend was repugnant.

"I know what I'll do," he said suddenly, "I'll have some teeth made out of it, too!"

The Pole stood up and held out his hand.

"Do whatever you like with it, Karl. Good luck to you."

Coward watched him go, too full to respond.

On their next visit to town, he steered the faithful Fritz toward a likely-looking dentist's parlor and produced before the startled gaze of the woman there an envelope of gold filings, taken, he explained, from rings bought from his fellow prisoners. The sight of sufficient money to pay quickly convinced her that a denture could be made; in due course it was ready, with a plate of gleaming yellow teeth the "Count's" impressive elegance was complete. The rest of the gold he kept prudently hidden.

In early June the order came to move. Their surprise gave way to anger when the cause became known. Apparently the Germans had taken to heart the pamphlets received from the United States Air Force and were evacuating the German staff from their comfortable quarters near the outside fence of the buna factory, with the intention of putting them in the British camp some three miles away. The Britishers were to occupy the German camp, and although the prospect of living in the clean and newly-built hutments was extremely pleasant, it was not so cheering to remember their proximity to a highly important target. However they were compelled to pack up their belongings and move. Coward straightway engineered a visit to Lamsdorf, ostensibly on other matters but really to protest through R.S.M. Lowe to the Red Cross in Geneva and from there to the War Office in London. While back in the huge camp he gathered all the latest news of the Normandy landings which had just begun and took it back to his men, joy in his heart. His own radio set had had to be dismantled for the move and the pieces distributed to dozens of men to carry in their effects. The Second Front was of course to all prisoners the most long-awaited and vital news of the war; there was tremendous jubilation among the Britishers at Auschwitz.

A month later came a heavy blow, robbing them of many friends and comrades.

Some of the men had organized a carnival on Saturday afternoon, to be followed by a show in the improvised theater of the new camp. Such an occasion gave full play to everyone's imagination; fantastic dresses were made and elaborate sideshows erected. There was a coconut shy, the "nuts" an ingenious construction of brown paper and cardboard, and a wobbly but effective miniature roundabout. One of the biggest "draws" was a bullfight between a corporal heavily attired in clothes meant to resemble those of a matador, and two men inside the paper skin of a "bull." It was a gala occasion, a chance to forget troubles and irritations, something to write home about.

No one bothered to dismantle the sideshows that evening; they were, in any case, the result of so much ingenious and laborious construction that it seemed entirely wrong to tear them down too quickly. Next morning, however, under orders from the Germans, the men gathered to reluctantly destroy their handiwork. The task had barely started when the sirens began to wail.

They were still wailing, and most of the men halfway to the shelters, when the first bombs fell.

17

INTO THE SLAVE CAMP

Coward came slowly to his senses. The air was full of noise, but it was all in his head. As the singing in his ears gradually receded, other sounds crept in, distant shouts and near at hand a groan of pain. He raised himself on an elbow and found that a thick pall of dust was blowing straight into his face. A few seconds passed before he realized the front of the hut was missing. Even then the full significance of what had happened did not dawn on him. He forced himself to his knees, then to his feet, and only a short and appalling scream snapped him into activity. Gripped with fear and horror, he stumbled over the debris on the floor and reeled outside into the dust cloud.

What he saw made him briefly and violently sick. The bombs had straddled the carnival ground, disintegrating the coconut shy and flinging the roundabout over on its side. Men were running toward the rough brick shelter, now half demolished with what appeared to be heaps of old clothes scattered about its entrance. He started to follow but tripped and fell. Looking beneath him he discovered part of a tunic, some of the blood in which it was soaked now transferred to his own battledress.

They recovered what bodies they could. The injured were laid in one of the remaining huts and comforted as far as possible until the arrival some time later of doctors from the nearest camps. Thirty-nine British prisoners died.

The entire surviving and unhurt contingent attended the mass funeral. Consumed by a deep and bitter rage, he hurried away as soon as the quiet and moving ceremony was over, insisting that he see the chief director of the Farben plant. The audience was granted, but he received scant sympathy.

"Your casualties are regretted," said the great man coldly. "All the Reich is now a target for your bombers. If they choose to be so indiscriminate in their attacks, I see no reason why you should expect to escape them. One may consider it," he added with venom, "a retribution for all the trouble you have been at pains to cause us."

Coward bridled. "What d'you mean by that?" he demanded.

"I am not a fool, neither are my codirectors. We are perfectly aware that you and your men have done all you can to disrupt production here. Without doubt you are responsible for certain acts of sabotage which have resulted in setbacks, though of a pathetically temporary nature."

Secretly delighted, but worried too, Coward decided to bluster. "That's a serious accusation," he returned hotly. "I'll report it to the Protecting Power and then we'll see what foundation you've got."

"Have no fear, Mr. Coward. We are also able to protect ourselves. Your little sport has come to an end."

"I have already lodged a protest with them against our men being kept here in danger of being killed."

"You surprise me, I should have thought that an inevitable hazard of serving in your gallant forces."

"You've no right to keep us in this hellhole!"

The director smiled thinly. "Let us not discuss rights, Sergeant major. Be grateful that you are still alive, but do not count on that happy state continuing indefinitely. Now get out. I will not be dictated to by an English guttersnipe."

Coward retired with as much dignity as he could muster. He had made his complaint and nothing more could be done. It was obvious that Farben had no proof to back their suspicions, but all the same he would have to be particularly careful in future.

Not so careful, though, that he hesitated to act when

there occurred to him the following week a quiet little scheme that would further delay production. The output of the factory was still relatively small for the size of the installations, largely due to the lack of a generating plant of sufficient capacity. The explosion engineered by the deportees had had invaluable effect, but since then a temporary generating plant had arrived and was almost ready to start up. All it required was the laying of cable in the ditches not so carefully dug by the British prisoners across miles of fields. Already the cable reached to the conduit leading inside the camp and the men were hard put to devise a way in which to delay completion. Then the idea came to Coward of cutting the cable as it was laid and disguising the breaks with clay and dirt to pass the inspection of the German electrical engineer in charge. To their glee, the scheme carried through without a hitch. The new plant, adjacent to the original site now wrecked, was duly connected and on the appointed day in August several dignitaries from Farben arrived to observe the ritual of starting the new source of power. Somewhat to his disappointment, Coward was absent, but according to eye witnesses the scene was very satisfactory. To the chief director himself fell the honor of throwing the switch, and he stepped back to share his colleagues' pride in their technical ingenuity. Nothing happened. He tried again. Sweating visibly, the German engineer checked the controls: everything seemed in order except for the conspicuous lack of current. The subsequent war dance performed by all present was a most interesting spectacle, not the least amusing aspect being their obvious indecision whether to confess the default to Berlin.

It took weeks of patient investigation to discover the breaks and as the work, given top priority, had been undertaken by parties from most of the camps, it was impossible to pin down responsibility. But Coward was under no delusion that he could fail to be the chief suspect and that one slip at this time would be fatal.

By now he had become expert in this form of sabotage. He also organized an escape club for the British, giving evening classes on the art and running a sweepstake on the chances of each individual man successfully breaking through the heavily guarded district. Once he caught sight of Goering and Goebbels making a lightning tour of the factory, grimly inspecting the results of their handiwork and regarding the half-dead workers around them with open contempt. They must have ordered an even greater impetus to the mass extermination conducted at Birkenau, for the damaged furnaces were speedily repaired and the numbers of the slain leaped skyward in the black and sickly smelling smoke. Perhaps in this later stage of the war they feared too many people remembering their infamy, but in Coward at least they failed utterly.

About this time a notorious gentleman left Birkenau for another command, and Coward, who knew him by sight and intimately by reputation, breathed a sigh of relief. No one, including the British, felt safe when he was near: his insatiable lust for blood was too strong for international law to deter. Major Kramer passed from the Auschwitz scene, leaving no regrets behind him. The only thing he left—and "thing" is an accurate term—was Irma Griese, that feminine beast who loved to strut around the various camps at Auschwitz wearing her well-tailored riding breeches and slapping a crop against her shapely legs. Her perversions were legion, yet in spite of the repulsion she aroused most of the wretches who saw her or who suffered the lash of her cruelty could not prevent an admiration of her beauty. That she was a lovely woman in her physical aspects was undeniable, but then so were Medusa and the Lorelei. In her body dwelt vices that only the testimony on oath of some of her victims make credible.

As the months wore on and the war seemed no nearer its end, so the Germans appeared to become more and more cruel, as if the shock of the Normandy landings had disappeared and they imagined the Allies would be permanently contained or thrown back. Then, in mid-September 1944, Coward was called

Irma Griese

upon to take his greatest risk and one that was to prove a deadly boomerang to his oppressors.

He was in the factory, exploring the possibility of reviving the escape scheme of using substituted bodies, and had been haggling with the *Unteroffizier* in charge of the cadavers. The man refused to take some of the gold Coward had left, and his prices in soap and cigarettes had risen steeply. Coward had told him to think again and was walking away, when he felt his sleeve pulled and looking down saw a small shriveled deportee imploring his attention.

"What is it, mate?" he asked.

"Pliz," whispered the slave painfully, "Pliz, Meester Coward, yes?"

"That's right, old man. I'm Coward." He felt in his pocket for a potato. He could never get used to the dumb despair and sheer misery of these poor people.

"I spik Englis' no good. Mus' talk."

"Yes? What's the matter?"

The man searched desperately for words. He seemed of Latin extraction, although it was difficult to be sure: after months of this hell all the slave workers became as one, all degraded to a common level. He twitched at his cotton pyjama tunic and looked about him nervously.

"Zere iss Englis' man . . . doctor . . . Birkenau. . . . He zay me spik you."

"Englishman!" exclaimed Coward gripping the man's bony shoulder and ignoring a *kapo* bearing down toward them. "Are you sure?"

"Yes, yes. He zick . . . zoon go . . . fire—"

He felt his stomach turn. "Bring me a note!" he almost shouted as the *kapo* swung his stick and the inmate sprawled to the floor, the potato rolling from his grasp. With a grunt the *kapo* made for it; his filthy hand crunched under Coward's boot. There was a yelp of pain and quickly, before the inevitable shout for a guard, Coward fished out a half-full packet of cigarettes; conquering his urge to vomit, he held them out. The *kapo* snatched at them, the eyes in his expressionless, dirt-caked face suddenly alive with greed. Magically rich beyond the dreams of avarice, he slunk away.

The hours until the next day seemed so intolerably long that Coward could hardly contain himself. If indeed there was a British doctor in the extermination camp, and one moreover who might soon be taken to the gas chamber, something would have to be done, and done immediately. To make representations to official quarters would obviously be a waste of time and might even ensure the man's death. Somehow, Coward must make contact with him, speak to him, get him out.

In the morning, when it came at last, he walked hurriedly through the factory, looking for the inmate who had approached him. Eventually he found the gang again, but the man was missing. He seethed for a few minutes, then on an impulse slipped the *kapo* more cigarettes and motioned him to walk a few paces away. The instant the *kapo's* back was turned, Coward felt a small ball of paper thrust into his hand. He turned, but the slaves around him seemed intent on their work. As casually as he could, he left the factory and then practically ran to his office; once inside, he spread out the paper, a strip torn from the edge of a newspaper yellowing with age, and stared at the faint scrawl of a pencil stub:

> *My name is ——, it ran, of—— Street, Sunderland. Naval doctor. Torpedoed. Jew. Separated from other British prisoners. Not allowed out working parties. Tell authorities and family.*

So it was true. He sat down slowly to think. He was still sitting there, his chin cupped in his hands, when the office door opened and the cheery face of Tich Keenan looked in.

"Oh, there you are, Charlie. Been looking for you all over the shop. We'll be late for the mail."

"You'd better get it yourself, Tich."

"Aye, aye—anything wrong?"

Coward passed him the note and watched the Cockney's eyes widen. "It's from the slave camp," he explained quietly.

"Blimey. You'd better take it to the personnel wallah, sharpish."

"Too dangerous. If he's in there, he's seen too much. They'd never let him out. Probably get rid of him straight away."

"What're you going to do then? Take it to R.S.M. Lowe?"

"I don't think there's time. I've been told he's sick and you know that means a 'transfer.'" Tich whistled. "In any case, R.S.M. Lowe would have to put it through official channels and as I say I think that's more dangerous than doing nothing."

"But you can't do nothing—"

"Who the hell said I'm going to do nothing?" Coward paused for a moment, lost in thought. "I've got to reach him somehow, talk to him. Then maybe I can smuggle him out."

"But he says he's not allowed out on working details."

"Yes, the swine are taking no chances with him."

"How're you going to talk to him, then?"

"I don't know. I just don't know. But I've got to do it, and fast." Coward got up and paced about the little room. "Just think, torpedoed, captured, brought here, roped into the Jews' camp—my God, what he must have been through. And now, if he's sick, he's probably heading for the gas chamber."

"The dirty rats. Surely they can't by law—"

"Yes, yes, yes. But all that takes time, and that's what we haven't got. I must get in to see him."

"Are you crazy? That's impossible."

"Nothing's impossible. I'll get in."

"But they'll never let you—"

"Don't be a bloody fool. Of course they won't, if they know anything about it. I don't propose to pin up a notice about it."

"What's the idea, then?"

"We know quite a lot of the inmates, because of the escapes we've organized. I'll meet up with them when they're coming back from working party and swap clothes with one of them."

"You mean, go in as a slave?"

"That's it."

Tich stood petrified for a moment. Then he burst out, "Now just a minute, Charlie—"

"It's the only way. I've made up my mind."

"Christ, you don't know what you're doing! Suppose you can't get out again—and what about the gas chambers—"

"It should be easy to find someone who'd like to spend a night in a real bunk with decent food to eat. I'll try to arrange it for tomorrow night. If I'm not back by the end of the following day, you can raise all hell."

"But Charlie, listen to me. Only a maniac would deliberately get into that place. You can't take the risk."

"Shut up!" Coward snapped testily. "If you were in his shoes, wouldn't you be hoping that someone had guts enough to try to help?"

"Well, yes, I suppose so, but—"

"Then for pity's sake pipe down and give me a hand." His irritation vanished as quickly as it had come and he grinned at his unhappy friend. "Scrub round it, Tich—you mean well, I know. But don't worry about me. I've looked after myself pretty well so far, haven't I?"

"You can do anything once too often."

"Too true. Write it down and hang it over my bed."

During the next day, while working with a digging detail, Coward had plenty of opportunity to get his hands and face thoroughly grimed. A little before six o'clock in the evening he mentioned to the *Feldwebel* in charge that it was necessary to visit another party before they dispersed for the day, turned up his coat collar to avoid unnecessary recognition, and made his way into the factory. Within a short time he was once more in the cellars, waiting.

It had not been difficult to find an inmate willing to

change identities for a night and enjoy a good rest. Approaching that inmate's particular *kapo,* a pock-faced brute who seemed more animal than man, was more nerve-wracking; for one dreadful instant, when he had grasped what was wanted, Coward had read in his beady, bloodshot eyes the idea of calling a guard and currying further favor by exposing the scheme. But the lure of cigarettes tipped the scales. For such a prize the *kapo* would have committed murder six times over; with the prospect of fifty, and a promise of twenty more cigarettes on Coward's safe return, his decision could not be in doubt. The man was not to be trusted an inch, but Coward felt he had made the bargain as watertight as he could and he hoped for the best.

Soon he could hear from overhead the shouted orders for the gangs of workers to form up for their march back to their camps. There were sounds of someone descending the stone stairs and he struck a match, revealing the inmate and his *kapo.* The cigarettes changed hands and he stripped off his clothes, reaching for the pyjama tunic; wearing it was like wearing nothing at all and he shivered as he helped the slave into his own heavy and unfamiliar clothes. The boots seemed to worry the man most; unaccustomed to their weight, he was panting by the time they reached the top of the stairs. The transformation, the wearing of real clothes for the first time in years, must have held all the qualities of a dream for him. Coward pressed his thin arm in reassurance and shoved him gently in the direction of the factory's main entrance, where a party of the boys would be waiting to smuggle him into the British camp.

In the crush of men who had appeared from their tasks like rats from their holes, no one had noticed. Coward turned to the *kapo* who, if he could think at all, probably judged him to be a lunatic, and muttered, "Come on then, you bastard. Let's get it over." With a sudden feeling of sickness he realized that the die was cast; discovery would mean death for himself, the inmate and the *kapo.* He began to stride after the *kapo,* then remembering his new identity, fell back to a scuffle, dragging his clogs along the floor and drooping his head. A light film of sweat broke out over his forehead.

They joined a gang of about fifty workers, all of them dressed in the same nightmarish suiting and waiting without impatience or any apparent feeling. A shout from the *kapo*, emphasized by indiscriminate blows on those nearest him, stirred them into shuffling activity. Jostling his way into the midst, Coward did his best to ape their movements, hanging his arms straight down and keeping his eyes on the feet of the man in front. His arrival occasioned no comment; indeed, most of the unfortunates seemed beyond speech. One or two stared at him with sunken, lackluster eyes, but with no real curiosity: if their eyes registered at all, they gave no sign.

Scarcely knowing where he was going, Coward became conscious of floorboards under his clogs. He looked up and found they were in a gloomy, dank washhouse; at least, so he supposed from the presence of three taps leaking a miserable trickle of water into sloping tin troughs. Some of the men made an effort to damp their hands and faces, but most of them just sank to the floor and sat or lay there without speaking. Someone belched and there was a faint, childlike titter.

The hoarse bellow of the *kapo* brought everyone struggling to his feet; they left the washhouse and resumed their march. Stealing a glance, Coward saw that they had entered the main camp. Long rows of wooden huts stretched out in streets on either side, paths of churned mud leading to the doors. Over all hung an indescribable odor.

A creature on one side of him began to lean against Coward's shoulder; even the weight of the skeleton of a man soon became an almost intolerable pressure, but gritting his teeth he made no attempt to move him. Before long there was a squelching underfoot, then they were filing through a door.

If the general smell of the camp had sickened Coward, that inside the hut hit him like a physical blow.

As his lungs sucked down the fetid air, compounded of filth and sweat and excrement, he felt a sudden panic of suffocation. He groped his way toward a broken window, braced himself against the wall, and tried to pierce the gloom: there were apparently no lights. Rows of three-tier bunks filled the hut, flimsy erections which swayed as the inmates leaned against them. He could see no furniture or blankets.

Apart from the almost obscene scuffling, like that of rats at the first coming of night, there were practically no sounds. Presently he heard an excited croak, followed by an animalistic scream making his scalp tingle. Two guards entered the doorway, behind them the spindly figures of two prisoners staggered with a small bin. They set it down and the *kapo* plunged in a tin mug to dole out a soup of unknown composition. The ration was evidently one bowl among six men; no sooner had each group drawn their portion than bedlam seized the hut. Coward made no move toward the bin —he doubted, in any case, his capacity to stomach the liquid—but stood appalled at the scene. Each man fought to get his fingers on the rim of a bowl; once he could get it to his lips he drank in frantic gulps until it was torn from him; long after it was empty he would struggle to get it back. Grunting, howling, choking in frustration, clawing and dragging with the puny strength of children, the prisoners of the Reich enjoyed their evening meal. Strutting in the doorway, the guards chuckled in high amusement. One of them nudged his companion and carefully aimed a kick with his jackboot at the back of a man who had at last gained temporary possession of a bowl. The blow cannoned the prisoner forward, shooting the remnants of soup on to the floor, the resulting uproar amply rewarding his tormentors.

On leaving the factory, and again before entering the camp, Coward's gang had been counted: now he could realize only too well why the slaves were often reputed to hold up the bodies of the dead comrades during these parades. Where food was so terribly meager, no method was to be spurned for gaining a little extra allocation.

Gradually the pandemonium subsided to a murmur and this phase of their entertainment over, the guards shouted *"Alles aus! Waschen!"* Coward surged forward with the rest: his eyes were now accustomed to the gathering darkness and looking down the length of the great hut he noticed for the first time two or three trestle tables but no chairs or forms.

As the place disgorged its human contents he was amazed to find an ever-growing crowd outside: well over a thousand men must have been crammed into it. Behind it in the mud a pole stretched across a noisome pit: this latrine proved to be the "ablutions." There was further diversion for the guards in watching the mob jostling for a turn at the pole before the fifteen-minute period expired. Coward moved in and out of the crowd asking in a desperate monotone if anyone knew the whereabouts of a British doctor: He received half-witted stares, blank looks of noncomprehension, smatterings of strange languages, an excited and unintelligible gabble from one wraith whose cheekbones threatened to burst their skin as he spoke, jerking his head with a violence that flecked the foam from his lips down on to his stubbled chin.

A whistle blew. In the ensuing scramble back to the hut, Coward was left well behind. At first he put this sudden haste down to fear of punishment from the guards or the *kapo*. As soon as he reentered the cavelike interior, however, the true reason became obvious. In a mad race made grotesque by their feeble strength the men were heaving themselves onto the swaying bunks, pushing and arguing for positions. Quickly every space was filled, three men to each bunk hardly wider than a shelf; lying half over each other, if one turned all would have to turn. He tried to grope about, intending to resume his questioning, but it was impossible to move without treading on those who were forced to lie on the floor. So he called out as loudly as he could, "British doctor! British doctor! *Wo ist?"*

He heard his own voice as in a nightmare; and might as well not have spoken. It was another sound in the jungle, without meaning.

For a while which may have been minutes but seemed eternity, he inched along feeling with his feet for a space to sit down, holding on to his nerves with every atom of his will power. Reaching down with his hands, he felt the faces of several men who were evidently sitting hunched up in a row; it was several seconds before it occurred to him that they must be up against a wall. Forcing one of them over, he edged in, lowered himself and sat with his knees under his chin, resting his head on his arms. The animal chorus of wheezes and groans receded in his exhausted brain.

Suddenly he snapped awake. Something moved over his hair. He brushed it off and a bony hand fell on his knee; thrusting it away, he struggled to keep down the bile in his mouth.

Dear God, he prayed, get me out of this—only get me out of this.

But the night was just beginning.

18

EXIT CHARLES COWARD

Half stifled by the atmosphere rancid with the stench of unwashed bodies, he made an attempt to compose himself for sleep, but it was impossible. The discomfort of his crouching position, the febrile mumblings of someone near him, the shock and fear of knowing he was in the very pit of the damned, prevented any chance of relaxing. He listened to the protesting creak of the bunks as occasionally inmates tried to turn in them, to the groans of those who suffered unconsciously in their sleep. As in other times of stress, he tried to fix his mind on what his family might be doing at home, but his little London house with its comparatively delicate furnishings belonged to a different life. In his mind rose the familiar image of a steaming hot meal set before him in a comfortable café and enjoyed to an accompanying chatter of discussion about the evening paper's sports news; it was fantastic, such things had never happened, would never happen.

For some time he could hear snatches of conversation conducted on one of the top bunks, catching nothing he could understand, simply following the pattern of the spasmodic, wooden tones. There were sounds of the soup bowls being used for another purpose and he realized with final humiliation that it was forbidden to leave the hut during the night.

After the war he was to be told accounts of how the three-tier bunks often collapsed under their loads. Those among the injured who were still conscious would be made to clean up the blood and were then taken away in the certain knowledge that with their working capabilities at least temporarily impaired, an appointment at the gas chamber was imminent.

As it was, on this particular night of his life which was never to be forgotten, there came a sudden cry from a high bunk, a heavy thump together with a sharp snapping sound, and then first one and then two appalling screams. Coward scrambled up, peering into the darkness to where a hubbub of voices had arisen, but nobody around about him moved. There were sounds of apparent accusation and argument, the whimpering of someone in pain. In a few moments the door of the hut swung with a crash and a raucous voice bellowed in German for silence. Somewhere an inmate started to say something; immediately there came the flashes and deafening intensity of two rifle shots. With hardly a pause the door was slammed to again. In horror Coward listened for the shrieks of the wounded to begin; there was a stunned quiet, unbroken even by the former whimpering, and he prayed that the bullets had been aimed at the ceiling.

The moans of the man who had fallen from his bunk returned, of course, within a few minutes and continued throughout the night, but they were one sound amongst many, arousing neither sympathy nor comment. Coward could feel the same numbness, not only of cramp, seep into himself; the urge to use his superior strength and force the men next to him to make more room was almost irresistible.

The night became a feverish mosaic, impossible to recall in detail, of terrified grunts as men started in their sleep, more door crashing and shouts from the guards, calls for a bowl or to God, words of anger which flickered fiercely and died suddenly. Doubled up as he was, every movement of the men beside him gave fresh pain. His body seemed alive with insects; the only replete form of life in the hut, their depredations raised lumps burning with irritation.

By the time the glass window had begun to frame the first pale light of dawn, he was incapable of feeling relief or thankfulness. He struggled blankly to his feet with the others when the guards came in, yelling and

laying about them with their rifle butts. They were soon
gone and the *kapo* took over, emerging from his crude
sanctorum to kick and beat into life those who were
not yet roused. Here and there an inmate made a
desperate but unsuccessful effort to hoist himself up;
when the *kapo* could see that blows from his stick
were useless, he would order the sick man to be
carried outside. A steady rain was falling as they formed
up for counting, the sick lying in the mud. Coward
wormed into the middle rank and stared at the ground
like his companions, only this time there was no pre-
tense. Saturated, cold, hungry, unutterably tired, his
back aching excruciatingly from the night-long crouch,
he felt completely spent, drained of will and even interest. For over an hour they stood in the rain while the
guards counted and recounted, prolonging the situation with relish. Occasionally a man fell down and
sprawled in his tracks, drawing scarcely a glance from
the guards or his fellows.

With the order to dismiss, when it eventually came,
began a fifteen-minute period to scrabble again for
the latrine pole, though always with a wary eye toward the guards. A minor infraction earned such pun-
ishments as having to carry four or five bricks wherever
one went, or trotting like a dog behind a guard as he
bicycled around the camp. Inevitably, a considerable
number failed to reach the pole, particularly those who
were weak from enteritis or dysentery and needed it
most.

Back in the hut, the brawl of the previous evening
was repeated as the bin of soup made its appearance.
Coward shuddered as he watched the unwashed bowls
put to their daytime use, snatched ferociously from
man to man. He sat and hungered for a cigarette.

The rest was a brief one, for they were soon being
herded out into the rain again to march to work. Feeling a little better now, though dreading that there might
be some hitch in his switching over to his own identity
(death seemed almost preferable to another night in
the camp), Coward looked covertly at the prisoners as
they began to walk. A poor fellow on one side of him

appeared more emaciated than it seemed a human being could become while still remaining alive, and the neglected sores of some disease of the skin covered his sallow face. The man shuffled on like an automaton, his eyes blank.

At the washhouse Coward this time took the opportunity to dampen some of his weariness away. He would need all his wits about him in five or ten minutes' time. The high point of danger came as they slowly approached the main gates; he hung his head as low as he could and guessed that the *kapo*'s fear must be as great as his own, for discovery could result only in instant death for them both. The queue moved gradually forward; he could hear the voices of the guards counting loudly. He was level with the gates, from whose arch bodies frequently swung in silent warning, then through. He breathed deeply and felt a great weight lift from him.

Other parties were already beginning to work as they entered the factory. He slipped from his rank and moved over beside the *kapo*, bumping into him as if by accident as they neared the cellar entrance. The *kapo* gave a barely perceptible nod and in the next instant Coward had whipped through the door and was clattering down the steps. There was no doubt in his mind that Tich would be waiting with the inmate, and he was right. Holding up a flickering match, the little Cockney gave him a wide, if anxious, grin of welcome.

"Thank 'eaven you made it, Charlie," he whispered. "Now for Pete's sake look slippy. He's all ready." He motioned the inmate at his side who was standing in underclothes. "There ain't much time, so move."

Stripping off the pyjama suit and wooden clogs, feeling again the warmth and cleanness of his own khaki and the familiar fit of his boots, Coward wanted to shout with delight. "Did he enjoy himself?" he spoke into the darkness as he did up his buttons. His arm was seized and a stuttering effusion of thanks, unmistakable though in a strange language, poured from the inmate. "Did you fix him up with fags, Tich?" he asked.

" 'Course, 'course. You all fit now?"

"Yes, but slip the *kapo* upstairs a packet, will you?"

"All right, but hurry!"

As they climbed the steps, he thought of the corpses dumped on the filthy stone floor and wondered how long it would be before the inmate behind him joined them. He pressed the fellow's hand, receiving a strong grip, one of new life and gratitude, and the picture of how the man would spend the next night brought a lump to his throat. He hardly noticed Tich's all-clear sign and waited unseeingly until his friend returned from a hasty negotiation with the *kapo*. They turned, and walked practically into an *Unteroffizier*. A wild panic seized him: surely they had been seen. He tried to say something and couldn't.

The German nodded and continued on his way.

"Blimey," breathed Tich. "Don't *do* that to me! Come on, let's get down to the boys."

In a corner of the huge yard to the factory, the British working party had just arrived on a digging detail. The two joined them unobtrusively, acknowledging a cautious wink of welcome, and took their places in the work. With his coat collar up and his face smeared with clay to hide his incriminating stubble from the guards, Coward worked with his men all day. Nothing about his escape was said until they regained the safety of the barracks that evening; then Tich threw his arms around him in a tremendous hug.

"You big galoot," he exclaimed. "How did you get on?"

"I got on all right," said Coward quietly. "Better than any of those poor bastards in there." He jerked a thumb over his shoulder, sat down on his bunk and accepted a cigarette. He leaned back, drawing the smoke deep into his lungs. Tich watched the bitter expression on his face and hesitated before asking, "Was it bad?"

"Bad, Tich? It was hell. Did you ever see any pictures of Dante's *Inferno?*"

"Christ, what's that, a disease?"

"I had a book once, when I was a kid. Never went

much on the poetry but there were drawings in it.
Never forgotten 'em. Skinny, naked people all fighting
each other in hell. Reckon that bloke must've known
something."

"That's what it was like, eh?"

"It's worse in there than anything you can imagine,
Tich. God knows how they keep alive at all. This is
the Ritz in comparison."

"Is it? I knew it reminded me of somewhere."

"If only the people at home could have some idea—
but they'd never believe it anyway. It's too terrible for
any sane person to believe unless he's seen it with his
own eyes."

"What about the doctor? Did you see him?"

Coward shook his head. "No, I didn't. Never even
found anyone who knew him. I tell you, Tich, there
are thousands and thousands of 'em in there. I never
stood a ghost of a chance, and neither does he."

Tich was silent, the full horror of it beginning to
dawn upon him. Then gathering himself, he jumped
up and got out the brewing-up tin.

"What we need is some good hot char. I'll cook
some meat roll and spuds. You look as if you could do
with some grub. Should've seen your oppo put it away
last night!"

"Oh yes, how did he get on?"

"He was in bleedin' fairyland. The boys dug up their
Red Cross parcels and we had a proper blow-out. None
of us could understand a word he said—didn't make
no difference. Gave him a damn good scrub first.
'Strewth, you should've seen his ribs."

"I've seen quite a few since yesterday."

"Sorry, yes. Then we kitted him out with under-
pants and vest—his face was a picture. D'you know I
could put my hand around his thigh? Never seen anyone so thin. When I gave him his plate of grub he grabs
me and gives me a real smacker on the cheek. Tucks
into it like he hasn't eaten for a year and then falls dead
asleep directly he's finished—we had to put him to
bed. Not used to it, I s'pose."

"You're not kidding, Tich."

"You'll feel better, too, as soon as you've got something inside you. Nothing like a spot of mother's good 'omely fare. All right, all right," he roared down the hut at the rows of listening Britishers. "Let's be having your tins. Bloody-well starving, the lot of you, I know. Monsewer Bloody Keenan, chef to perishing Auschwitz, that's me."

The strained look gradually went from Coward's eyes and he slowly reverted to normal. After the meal they trooped off to the little theater that had been prepared at the bottom of one of the huts and saw a dance band on the diminutive stage. One of the tunes had been written by the versatile sergeant major and it cheered him up to hear it. But later on in the shelter of his bunk, dreams of the slave camp returned to haunt him; several days passed before the memory of that dreadful experience sufficiently dulled for him to be his usual lighthearted self.

He was acute enough to notice, as the months rolled slowly on their course, that a new vigilance, a special watchfulness, had crept into the manner of the Germans surrounding him. For one thing, they changed his personal guard very frequently and seldom now did he have his old watchdog, Fritz. Instead a new succession of keen eyes and younger Fritzes made their appearance, soldiers who were adamant in their objections to his doing anything or going anywhere that might cause the slightest infringement of the rigid rule applying to a British Man of Confidence. The new guards seemed impervious to bribes; although they accepted cigarettes and chocolates with the usual alacrity, they would allow no relaxation of the rules in return. He was obliged to abandon his attempts to win them round and restricted his activities to the escape classes and the little acts of sabotage in which he loved to indulge. It was very much harder, too, to get back to Lamsdorf, even on Red Cross affairs. The Germans made various excuses for stopping him going, but they all amounted to the same thing: that he was being carefully watched and his actions severely circumscribed. He was accused of nothing, but there was an underlying suspicion that he was up to something.

The first intimation of trouble came when a British prisoner arrived from Lamsdorf, bringing him a note from the camp leader. Short and to the point, it told Coward that for some time the Germans had suspected him of sabotage and of having some connection with the Polish Underground. Investigations by the *Gestapo* had ferreted out the fact that on the night of the raid on the photographer's shop in Auschwitz a break had been found in the wire around the British camp, yet no prisoner had been reported missing. From this they deduced that he might have been at the shop and escaped with the incriminating evidence which they had failed to find. It was imperative that he leave the area and he would be posted forthwith to a working camp at Teschen.

The information was not entirely unexpected and he set about covering his tracks. Luckily Fritz had just left to join a battalion on the Eastern front, so he was at least temporarily out of the way. Everyone who had known of his activities was warned to keep a tight mouth, not only for his sake but for their own.

Only two days passed before he was told gruffly by the *Unteroffizier* in charge of his barrack that he was to move immediately to Teschen, a camp some twenty miles to the northeast. Expressing surprise, he packed his bag at once. The next morning he was gone, this time under the wing of two guards whose stiff bearing brooked no familiarities, leaving his friends and a downcast Tich behind him. Although he was sorry to part company with so many true comrades, he could feel no spasm of regret at saying goodbye to Auschwitz. Looking back from the train as it steamed out of the station, he could see the five chimneys smoking furiously, casting their load of human ashes on the autumn air, a black monument of the inhumanity of man. Again he vowed to himself that the reckoning must come.

Teschen was reached after several hours and he found a further shock awaiting him. After the inevitable search he was let loose into the main body of the camp and sought out the camp leader to introduce himself and find a bed. As often happened, the leader turned out to be a sergeant major whom he had known fairly well at Lamsdorf. The man greeted him somewhat lugubriously.

"Hello, Charlie. Sorry to see you here."

"Well, that's a fine welcome," returned Coward. "What the blazes d'you mean, sorry to see mc here?"

"Got bad news for you, boy. Looks as if Jerry has twigged your little lark or something."

"Why, what's up?"

"Well, the *Feldwebel* here has told me you're to be moved on Saturday to the interrogation center in Berlin. You know what that means, don't you?"

Coward grimaced. He knew only too well what it meant. A Berlin interrogation showed that the Germans' suspicions must have hardened into certainty and they intended to grill him until he came out with the truth. That way spelled curtains.

"Blind old Pete," he muttered. "That's torn it."

Gregory, the camp leader, looked at him hard.

"I don't know what you've been up to, you silly bastard," he said heavily, "but whatever it is, you've led them a rare old dance. The *Feldwebel* was saying the heads are pretty worked up over it."

Coward lit a cigarette and tried to think. He was on the run indeed, from the *Gestapo* this time, yet what could he possibly do? It seemed that the Germans had him cornered. Yet Gregory looked unperturbed. He shuffled through a pile of papers on his desk, nominal rolls, ration indents, sick lists.

"If you ask me," he went on, "you'd better quietly disappear. The war looks as though it's on its last legs now and you might make it."

"How the hell can I do that? They know I'm here."

" 'Course they do. But you'll have to disappear just the same. I'll put you down on this list of men going out to the mines in Bobrek tomorrow morning. You can join them as Private—er—Johnson. You can take up duties as assistant to the Man of Confidence over there. T.S.M. Powell is his name, Sandy to his pals. Nice bloke. You'll like it."

Coward could have kissed him.

"You're a wizard, Greg!" he exclaimed. "But d'you think they'll spot me?"

"Don't see why they should," said the older man thoughtfully. "You'll have to take the scrambled egg off your sleeves, of course. I think I can fix the rest. Y'see, we've been covering up for Johnson ever since he escaped over a month ago, so as the Jerries don't know that he's not here you can take his place. The only point is, of course, that B.S.M. Coward will have to be put down as missing, believed escaped, and won't be seen any more."

Coward did not hesitate. "Right, I'm on! It's Private Johnson as from now."

"You'd better kip down in here for tonight, Charlie. Keep out of sight and be ready to move first thing in the morning."

His host provided him with a cup of tea and then he set about the task of destroying all traces of Sergeant major Coward. All names on his clothes were blacked out, his insignia of rank removed, and what papers he possessed heavily camouflaged to hide his real name. Gregory produced a spare identity disc which was laboriously carved by one of the prisoners with Johnson's name and number, and this Coward hung around his neck. In his pocket he put a letter from Gregory to T.S.M. Powell, explaining the switch-over in the prisoners' rough and ready code and asking him to use what influence he could to keep the Germans away from Coward.

All was ready, and when the party walked through the thick raw morning mist to board the waiting lorries, Coward was with them.

He found no bother in getting through the searches on leaving Teschen and on arrival at Bobrek and was

soon confronting the famous Powell, a tall and somewhat elderly soldier of the old school who immediately
sized up the situation and welcomed him warmly. It
was not the first time that he had accomplished this sort
of thing.

"You'll work here in my office," he explained. "I
can do with a bit of a hand, anyway. The lads work in
the mine, but that's not so bad as it sounds. It's a proper mine, you know. Goes into the side of the hill.
Good coal, too."

Coward chuckled. "Stuff the coal, Sandy," he said.
"What chances of a moonlight flit here. Any?"

Powell clicked his tongue. "You'll be a bloody fool
if you try that on, son," he answered reprovingly. "In
the ordinary way I'd say go ahead and good luck to
y', but with your record and going under an assumed
name too, it'd be fairly asking for it. No, you let that
alone."

"Okay, you're the boss," said Coward disconsolate-
ly, realizing that Powell was perfectly right. "I'll be
good. What's happening to the war? D'you know?"

Powell told him the news over a brew of coffee,
and heartening it was. On the western front, the Allies
were poised on the brink of a big push. In Italy, that
grim battlefield among the olive trees and vineyards,
only the northern-most section remained in German
hands: the Allied thrust had deliberately slowed, containing as many enemy troops in the area as possible.
As for the enormous Red Army, its pressure was now
so great that it was only a matter of time before it
reached this very camp.

So, with over-optimism, they yarned and counted
the days.

It was quite a pleasant period for Coward. True,
Red Cross parcels began to get few and far between
and then abruptly stopped altogether, but the encouraging news compensated for that loss. All the same,
Christmas seemed a bleak prospect without any food
extras, and the more depressing because all of them
had expected in rosy anticipation to be home by then.

Even Coward's usual buoyancy failed him when Christmas Day dawned and saw them still enclosed within that eternal barbed wire with the empty Polish landscape surrounding them. Snow had fallen thickly and the cold was more intense than had been known even in those parts for many years.

The day was a hungry one for them all, but some of the men had managed to smuggle in a few bottles of beer and wine. An impromptu show was held in one of the barracks and for a few hours they forgot themselves in horseplay and rousing choruses. Situated actually inside the mine yards, the camp was overshadowed by huge humps of slag and coal that looked down like white-haired old gentlemen on the prisoners as they sang. Coward looked out at the heaps, idly tracing their outline against the gray sky, wondering if Scouse and Barney and the others were having a good time, trying to imagine what presents his children at home would have received from their mother. He found himself staring harder. Over the top of one of the heaps a light appeared to be flickering, growing stronger, then dying out. Another sprang up, a little to the right, looking for all the world like an army flare. Perhaps the Germans were on maneuvers. Or—his heart leapt. He jumped to the window and stuck his head out. In a lull in the singing, he heard a distinct rumble, low and constant in the distance.

"Boys, boys!" he yelled. "I can hear the guns!"

In a moment, everyone was on his feet. Scattering chairs to right and left, they swarmed out into the compound and listened. The mutter and grumble of far-away artillery bombardment came clearly to them in the still air.

"It's the Russkis, the flippin' Russkis!"

Cheering madly, they cavorted up and down the compound, shouting messages to Uncle Joe and Hitler, dancing, slapping each other on the back, beside themselves with joy.

"We're free, me old chinas!" bellowed someone. "It's good old Blighty for us in a few hours!"

"What about that pint at the Red Lion, Bill?"

"Look out, Pompey! Get up them stairs!"

In all that they had gone through, they should have known better.

19

THE ALLIES COME

Disillusionment was swift. At dawn the very next morning there were shouts from the guards for everyone to be ready to parade within five minutes for rollcall: they would march immediately. When the Allies were fighting in the very streets of Berlin some five months later, the German High Command would not admit defeat. Now, in the last few days of 1944, they were certainly hopeful of a reverse in their favor and all prisoners of war were therefore to be removed as far from the fronts as possible.

The men hastily dressed in their warmest clothing, packed what they could in the way of kit and spare food, and lined up outside for the usual count. Coward fidgeted in the snow. He fluently cursed all Germans, as indeed all the men were doing in their disappointment. As the *Feldwebel* made his way slowly along the lines, counting, some of the prisoners tried the time-honored delaying tactic of dodging about, but his revolver quickly discouraged such games. All the time the rumble of guns was distinctly audible and in the men's imagination seemed appreciably nearer. But it was no good. Soon after nine o'clock they started to march, out of the camp and along the white-covered roads, trudging through the piled-up snow and heading straight into the teeth of the wind. Coward walked alongside Sandy Powell for a while, helping him to keep the men in a compact bunch. Too many stragglers might well have induced the guards to adopt their usual measure: shoot anyone who dawdled, as so much expendable material.

All over Germany and the occupied countries men and women in the thousands were beginning what the English newspapers described as "The Death March," trekking through the snow away from the terrible onslaught from the East. As the Red Army advanced further and further, not only prisoners of war were forced to flee in front of them but also immense numbers of civilians, deported people who had been brought from their different homelands to work in the eastern cities of Germany, Poland and neighboring countries. All marched inexorably westward. What would happen when the other Allies entered Germany from the west, nobody seemed to know or care; there was a general reluctance to be dormant in the path of the Russians.

Eyed closely by the guards, the men from Bobrek trudged on and their march, which at the outset they had assumed to be probably a few hours, took steady toll of the days and then the weeks. Their direction seemed haphazard: the *Wehrmacht* major who led the column appeared to have no definite instructions, sometimes drastically changing their course according to where he heard the Russians were breaking through. There were no issued rations and the men began to slowly starve; in those near-Arctic conditions it was not easy to scavenge vegetables from the fields and the years of malnutrition soon began to tell; men suddenly collapsed and were left behind. They would pass bodies lying by the wayside, usually Russian prisoners who had been shot by their guards while on the march, and once they passed through a village where a heap of dead horses lay beneath a sign that read *Wir danken unserem Führer*. It brought many an ironic remark from the endless columns streaming past it. *Thank you, Führer* was just a trifle out of place now, even to the most fanatic of Nazis.

Coward managed fairly well, keeping company for most of the way with Sandy Powell. Owing to the impossibility of washing or shaving he now possessed an incipient beard. Beneath his balaclava helmet he looked like an Arctic explorer, and indeed felt like one too. Continual sleeping out in the freezing fields or in barns wet with thawed snow had given him a cough that racked him through and through, but in spite of this and other inconveniences he managed to keep most of the men remarkably cheerful. Starving though they were, they knew that the days of the German State were numbered.

Toward the end of January, what was left of the column arrived weary and footsore at a large camp somewhere in the south of Germany. It was a dismal place into which men of many nationalities were herded like so many sheep, but it held a spark of interest for the new arrivals, for here were hundreds of American prisoners of war who had been captured in the fighting in France. Their natural ebullience seemed unimpaired at this sudden transition from the comparatively well-fed and decent conditions of warfare prevailing under an American Command, to the filth and squalor of such a huge prison camp. Coward made firm friends with several of them, impressed by their generosity and unshakable spirits. When he first stumbled into one of the barracks there, prepared to sleep blanketless on the concrete floor, he was taken under the wing of Hank and Johnny from Chicago and Detroit respectively. They told him to share their bunks with them and although they were in a bad way themselves, gave him half of what was left of their rations. This consisted of a slice of iron-hard bread and two sardines, but it did more to Coward than stave off immediate starvation.

Not long after their arrival at this camp, where the daily issue amounted to a tenth of a loaf and a few potatoes, the astonishing fact became known that the German *Kommandant* was raising prize rabbits in his garden. Without ado Coward and two British prisoners, a lad from Johannesburg and a Geordie, carried out the necessary sortie. The incredible risks entailed in dodging the searchlights to cross two wire fences in the dead of night, and then tramping around afterward to destroy the footprints in the snow that would lead investigators straight to their huts, were more then worthwhile when they thought of the delicious stew to be enjoyed. It was a lengthy operation and Coward had no sooner deposited himself on the edge of Hank and Johnny's bunk, one of the rabbits rolled inside his battledress, when three guards stumped in, shouting that some swinehound had stolen the *Kommandant's* pets. He hastily thrust the creature under the pile of coats that did service as a pillow and sat, all innocence, to await developments.

Slowly the soldiers moved up the hut, looking for the telltale traces of blood or fur. Billy Jordon, the South African, had managed to drop his precious loot into the snow outside the glassless window, poking it well down into a drift, but Coward was caught, literally, red-handed. As the Germans came abreast of him he looked up at them mildly, his hand resting gently on the bundle of clothes beneath which lay the dead rabbit. Dead? He thought he had killed it, but suddenly he felt it move. He tried to grip it, but it squirmed under his touch. Despite the subzero temperature, he began to feel exceedingly warm.

The guards looked at him suspiciously, he yawned rather ostentatiously and leaned even more heavily on the rabbit. It bucked and tried to jump. He cleared his throat loudly and started to whistle. When, with a final glare, the guards moved on into the next barracks he was damp with perspiration.

"Oh, blimey. Thought that was my lot."

It was a gloriously comforting feast to which his American friends were invited the following night.

Time hung heavily on their hands there; they had little to do but nurse their hunger and wait for the end of things. Although the camp lay well inside Germany, it was obvious that the Germans could not keep them there if they intended avoiding their recapture. Guarding so many of them with the small number of posterns under his command was a great headache for the *Kommandant:* each of the barracks was crammed to overflowing, several men sharing one bunk that was normally inadequate for one. The general mood was bad and it became dangerous for a German to enter the huts. With the thaw came the mud, quickly churned to quagmire. Many of the men who had developed frost-bite on the march experienced agonies when they tried to walk about. The few doctors and medical orderlies who had stuck with the men all along did wonders in their attempts to heal the sick, but aspirin and a few paper bandages comprised the entire medical supplies and did little to ease the suffering.

At this time Coward's thoughts were very much of home. After the rabbit episode, he was very circum-spect, very good now, taking the line that having come so far and suffered so much it would be foolish to further risk his life in any way. Nevertheless, he some-times talked escape with the Americans, answering their eager questions on the best ways and means. Both Johnny and Hank were in their nineteenth year and he felt old enough to be their father.

In March, with the guns booming once again in the distance, came the long-expected order to pack up and parade outside. They were given one loaf each, briefly counted in the pale sunshine, and then ordered to start moving.

"Here we go again," he groaned.

His belongings had by this time shrunk to a hand-kerchief and his shaving tackle, so at least he could travel light. Off went the column, bigger than ever now.

Day after day they marched slowly along, all of them tired unto death, the spirit oozing out of them. They had been at starvation level for three months and this extra marching was the last straw. The men be-came weaker and weaker, the guards touchier and touchier. At night they were crammed into barns, fac-tories, cowsheds, anywhere that could provide any semblance of shelter. One night Coward spent his sleeping hours in a milking plant with his head under-neath a cow, in imminent danger of being trod on or rolled on. Another night was spent upon piles of sacks containing residue from sugar beet. This was a wind-fall, for they found that by chewing the residue they could extract a reasonable amount of sugar, and this warmed and fed them.

Then late one night they arrived at a small village somewhere in the heart of the Reich and the officer leading the column sought out the *Bürgermeister* to en-quire where the men could be sheltered. An excited old gentleman appeared from the *Bürgermeister's* house, gesticulating wildly and babbling furiously in German. The officer looked appalled, then turned rapidly around. He barked an order and the entire column of prisoners, many thousands of them, turned about and marched out of the village again. Eventually they were led off the road and into what appeared to be an exten-sive quarry; tools still littered the ground where the evacuated workmen had left them. A few guards stood at the entrance to the quarry and as the head of the column, which included Coward, made its way into the great artificial canyon, one of them called out iron-ically, "See you in the morning!"

Something queer about this, he thought, looking up at the steep walls of the cutting. Then, quite clearly in the moonlight, he caught sight of a tiny hut at the far end, and breaking away from the men he hurried over to it. Inside were a dozen or so Americans, some crouching, several sprawled out on the wet ground and obviously dead. For a moment he was too sur-prised to speak. Then he called out:

"What's the matter, blokes? Anything we can do?"

One of them waved at him and croaked:

"Get the hell out. Don't come over here. It's typhus. They've left us here to die."

Typhus! It needed only this. He doubled back, call-ing out for volunteers to help. Hank and Johnny came forward, thin and pale though they were themselves, and five or six other men. The little party went over to the American sick and did what they could for them, although that was practically nothing. Four were al-ready dead and it could be only a matter of hours for the rest. A deep bitterness filled Coward's heart as he wiped the face of the boy who lay at his knees, so young to die so far from home. He listened to the feverish calls for the dear ones and the night was filled with lonely horror.

By morning it was all over. None of the sick men had survived, but perhaps their last moments had been made just slightly better by the Britishers and the two Americans who were with Coward. He found some picks and shovels in the hut and organized a burial party, laying the thin bodies reverently in the shallow graves and saying a simple, downright prayer over their tombstones of heaped-up rocks. Their end, at least, came with dignity and compassion.

There were three more days to be spent in the quarry, everyone growing steadily weaker. By some miracle, none of them contracted the dreaded disease that had carried off the Americans, and perhaps because of this the Germans let them out and formed them up again for the march. It seemed impossible that they could walk farther, but they did, eating the grass that was now flourishing by the roadside and raiding potato clutches in the fields, twisting with the pains of acute hunger.

Coward kept doggedly on, trying not to think now, pushing thoughts of home resolutely to the background. Before he could get home, to his wife and children, home to the little pub around the corner and to the pictures in the High Street, he had to get out of this mess, out of this eternal marching, marching, marching. Like everybody else, he had lost a good deal of weight and was ravingly desperate for food. All his strength was concentrated in the effort to keep moving, keep moving, to watch the feet of the men in front and keep up with them.

Once he grinned feebly at Hank, hobbling along beside him.

"How goes it, old son?" he asked.

The tall, lean American boy lifted a haggard face and smiled at him with cracked, dry lips.

"Fine, fine. How's it yourself, Charlie?"

"Not so bad. Can't last for ever, can it?"

"So they tell us. Me, I think it's that long already.

You wouldn't have another rabbit tucked away, would you?"

"We might find something. Hang on a bit longer."

"Say, who're you giving the treatment? I'm good for another couple of hundred miles before these Heinies rest up for a smoke. How many years is it since we had the last break, anyway?"

"Don't ask me. I traded my watch long ago."

"Me too. But what the hell, time's nothing. Doesn't matter any more. Kind of crazy when I think how I used to fly around trying to snick off a minute here and there."

"What did you do in Civvy Street?"

"Oh, I was fresh out of college, just starting in my old man's motor business and ready to go places."

"You'll go back to that, I suppose? Sounds good."

"How would I know what I'll do? It was a good life, I know that now. Goddammit, after what I've seen over here, I'll really appreciate the States. But I don't know, I guess it's me for the quiet life when this is over."

"We all feel like that. A chance to live your own life for a while. You're not married?"

"No. But there was a girl—I hear from her once in a while. Maybe we'll shack up, she's a good kid. Seems kind of important now to have a home of your own. Can you imagine it? Do whatever you want. Live like decent human beings. Yeh, we might even let our kids grow up and die of old age." Embarrassed, he stopped himself. "Guess I'm sounding off."

They could not know it, but the end was nearly in sight. Dirty, worn out and scarcely recognizable, they had stumbled through to the end of the war.

20

ESCAPE, SEVENTH AND LAST

They made it to Hanover. Staggering through the streets, they looked with wonder at the colossal damage wreaked by the R.A.F. blockbusters the night before. The railway station was a shambles and in the big marshalling yard outside not a clear line had been left. Gangs worked frantically on the twisted tracks, while cranes lifted smashed and burnt-out rolling-stock on to huge piles of rubble. It was clear to Coward that Germany was dead as a country, but would not give up until the madman at the helm was exterminated. Scraps of news were gleaned from passers-by, indicating that the American and British armies could not be far away. It was an exulting thought, filling the prisoners with renewed life as they conjectured on the chances of being liberated by their own people.

Picking their way through the ruins, they came to rest in a school. This was haven indeed. Once inside, with guards stationed around the building, they commenced to break up the furniture for firewood. Following an announcement from the guards that they could expect only half a loaf of bread a day, and perhaps not even that, a hurried Council of War was held to decide how they could augment their food supply. Coward presided and put to the meeting that the most important task before them was to get word through to the Allied Forces. He and three others volunteered to make a break for it at the earliest possible moment, but with the school in the position of a beleaguered garrison, the guards having orders to shoot at sight, the problem was a difficult one.

A week passed, seven nights of cowering under the fury of the R.A.F.'s attacks, before an opportunity occurred. Opposite the school stood a large house in its own grounds, obviously the residence of someone of wealth. At dusk one evening a group of prisoners lounged in the doorway to the school, gazing longingly at the gates and beyond them to the house across the way, when one of the men noticed a thin spiral of smoke rising from an upper window. It was enough.

"Fire!" shouted Coward at the top of his voice. He ran over to the two guards at the main gate. *"Feuer, Feuer!"* he roared, waving his arms madly in the true German manner and pointing wildly at the house. The guards looked startled and in their indecision made a false step. "Come on!" exclaimed one of them and made a bolt for the house, his whole thoughts concentrated on dousing the fire before darkness fell and the cursed R.A.F. arrived.

His companion followed, and after him a stream of prisoners, forgotten in the heat of the moment. Closely pursued by one of his friends, Harry Allingham from London, Coward plunged into the house on the heels of the guard. Two astonished German civilians emerged from an upper room as the party came clattering up the stairs, a man who immediately joined in as he heard the magic word *"Feuer,"* and a woman who promptly fainted away. Ever the gentleman, Coward dumped her into a chair before turning his attention to the rest of the house. While the guards and sundry helpers were smothering the flames in one bedroom, he and Harry ransacked the wardrobes of another. Quickly they stuffed under their arms the first male clothes to hand and dashed downstairs and through to the back of the house. Fairly whooping with joy, they snatched up bread, sausage, cheese and a bottle of *schnapps* from the pantry, crammed them into their pockets, and made off down a side street, running hard. Altogether, some twenty prisoners escaped in the mêlée and it may be suspected that their riddance was welcomed by the Germans at the time: their presence was certainly an embarrassment.

It was lucky that the school was on the outskirts of the town, for the two Britishers could not have run far. As it was, within a few minutes they found themselves on the edge of a patch of allotments.

"Quick," gasped Coward. "Get into one of the huts."

Among the gardening tools and flower pots they changed clothes, viewing each other with complacency despite their lack of collars and ties. Coward sank gratefully into a wheelbarrow that stood in one corner.

"We might as well sleep here tonight and push on tomorrow," he said. "We can take the barrow and push it along the streets until we get out of town. Look better that way. You can get anywhere in the world with a ladder on your shoulder, so I suppose it's the same with a barrow."

The food in their pockets made a delicious meal, the first real one they had tasted for weeks. They were cautious in sampling the *schnapps:* in their weak state, it might have had a disastrous effect. Squeezed side by side into the barrow, they dozed off, comfortable and content. It was not a cold night and they slept well, so well that only the creaking of the door aroused them.

In the daylight an old man stood looking down at them his lower jaw sagging with shock. The Britishers stared back at him in sleepy vacancy. Then Coward struggled up and seized the old man's arm.

"Look, Dad," he said. "Sorry to scare you but I'm afraid you'll have to stay in here for a bit until we get away. Savvy?"

The old man's eyes popped at the words.

"*So? Engländer, ja?*" he wheezed.

"*Ja,*" chipped in Harry. "*Viel Engländer kommen hier, morgen frei.*" He gestured expansively, conveying that the whole countryside was literally overrun with the invading armies.

"*Yoy!*" muttered the old man weakly, beginning to tremble.

Coward gathered up his bits and pieces of food and stuffed them back into his pockets.

"Come on, Harry. We're off," he said maneuvering the barrow out. He turned back to the very shaken owner. "You'll have to do your weeding without this, mate. Be a good boy now," and a gentle shove deposited the ancient among the flower pots, where he sat open-mouthed in astonishment and fear.

The barrow's rusty wheel squeaking in protest, they set off at a brisk pace heading away from where they imagined the center of town to be. Remarkably few people were about and they realized that most of the civilians must have moved out ahead of the impending battle. The sounds of gunfire seemed very close.

"There's no sense in going too far," said Allingham, "or sooner or later we're bound to run into the Jerry rearguard."

"You're right. We'd better look out for an empty house and lay up."

They wandered around, taking it in turns to push the barrow. Suddenly Allingham exclaimed "Watch out!" as a German staff car turned a street corner ahead and came toward them.

"Grab these bricks," snapped Coward, jumping up on to a pile of masonry and industriously heaving chunks of it down into the barrow. The car crept past them, bumping slowly over the debris.

"Can't take any more chances," said Coward, promptly emptying the barrow again. "First likely-looking house we see."

They found one on a corner, standing a little apart from its neighbors. Nothing remained of the windows and it was an easy matter to climb in. Fragments of wood and glass littered the floors inside but a divan bed in the living room was intact and on its soft mattress they stretched themselves luxuriously.

"This is a bit of all right," said Allingham drowsily, munching his remnants of bread and cheese.

Coward agreed. "Not bad at all, Harry boy," he mumbled. "But it's pretty damn quiet round here. I don't like it."

"I do. Let's have a kip."

They were still sleeping when night came and whatever terrors it might have held were completely lost on them. It took a thunderous explosion to bring them upright, dodging a shower of plaster from the ceiling. Coward leaped to the window and peered out into the early morning light.

"Holy smoke, there's a Jerry tank right outside the perishing house and he's belting away like stinko up the road."

As Harry joined him at the window the gun roared again, the conclusion sending them reeling back. The house rocked from the blast of nearby shells. Right under their noses, so it seemed, a machine gun began to chatter with nerve-wracking loudness.

Coward sat down on the bed again.

"Knew there wasn't enough noise," he said and took a swig from the bottle of *schnapps*. "Well, all we can do is sit tight and hope for the best. I'll make a bloody strong complaint if we get bumped off after coming all this way."

They finished the bottle as the battle intensified, retiring under the divan when the house next door partly collapsed. Bullets snicked against the outside walls and one screamed in through a window, disintegrating a massive and hideous china vase.

"Damn it, that would have been handy." Coward snuffed trying to blow bed fluff from his nostrils.

Fortunately, the engagement was short. Toward afternoon the noise retreated to the distance and they stepped warily to the window again. Nobody was in sight, though a thick pall of dust prevented them from seeing very far.

"Think it's safe to start moving?" wondered Allingham.

"We'll have to. Let's see if the barrow is still there and then get weaving."

That trusty piece of hardware was still in the front garden where they had dumped it. Coward seized the handles and they made their way slowly down the brick strewn road.

"Look," he nodded. "It's had a fair bashing round

here since yesterday. Lots of work for us to do, clearing up this mess."

At the corner they halted, uncertain which way to go.

"Better toss for it," suggested Allingham.

"What with—a button? Come on, we'll try down here."

Like two extremely decrepit rag-and-bone merchants they moved forward again, clattering noisily over the rubble in their path. Instantly a voice shouted:

"Hey, you!"

They stopped and looked up and down the road.

"Funny," said Coward. "Could have sworn I heard someone call."

"Me too. Must be getting the willies."

"Noises in the blooming head now? Come on."

Two more paces and the voice bellowed again:

"I said you! Stay where you are!"

"Don't tell me I imagined it that time," said Coward. He called out, "Where are you?"

"So you speak English, huh? Come over here."

"Where?" shouted Coward, thoroughly irritated.

"Here, goddammit!" the voice positively thundered.

Coward glanced up and jumped. Protruding through what remained of the front of the house yawed the snout of an enormous tank. Astride the top of it like a man in a recruiting poster, his belt strung with grenades and his carbine pointing unwaveringly at them, stood a begrimed G.I.

"Blimey!" ejaculated Coward. "The man from Mars!"

They stumbled over toward him.

"Hold it, hold it! Keep your hands high."

The soldier swung lithely down and then stepped hastily back as Coward rushed to shake his hand.

"Not so fast, you! What is this?"

"Gosh, are we glad to see you—"

"Yeh, yeh. I had that treatment before. Hey major!" shouted the G.I. Then to Coward, "Don't tell me. You speak English, you love Americans, you hated the

Nazis. Brother, that line went out with long pants."
He spat disgustedly.

"Wait a minute. We're British."

"From London," put in Allingham.

"That's right—both of us," added Coward.

"We've been waiting for you to get here—"

"Hiding out round the corner—"

"So you walk around in civvies with a wheelbarrow looking for me," said the G.I. "Oh sure. Dumb of me not to know. *Major!* Where is that sonofa—"

He broke off as a tough-looking individual, bristling with armament, emerged from the shell of a house opposite.

"Jeez, major, I been yelling for half an hour—"

"Okay, okay. What's happening here?"

"We're British, sir," called Coward as the officer approached, eyeing them grimly.

"Where did you flush these?" he demanded of the G.I.

"Just wandering down the road here. With a wheelbarrow."

"Wheelbarrow! What the—"

"It was camouflage, like," explained Coward. "I'm Sergeant major Coward—that is, the Jerries think I'm Private Johnson—"

"I'm Eisenhower too. What're the glad rags for? You deserters?" barked the American.

"Deserters?" stuttered Coward, mortally insulted. "Listen, we're prisoners of war. Escaped. We've been laying up waiting for a chance—"

"You got your identity tabs?"

They slipped off the metal discs from around their necks and handed them over.

"Uh-huh. No names—just your *Stalag* number. Well, we can check on that, I guess. What's your name, son?" to Harry.

"Allingham—Private Allingham, sir."

"And yours?"

"The identity number belongs to a Private Johnson—that's who the Jerries think I am—"

"Do they now? And who do *you* think you are?"

"I told you—Sergeant major Coward. I was in a spot of trouble and the *Gestapo* were ready to take me in, so I let them think I'd escaped and swapped identities with Johnson because he'd already escaped, you see."

"Damned if I do. Anyway," turning to the G.I., "you'd better radio up the lieutenant to get a jeep along here." He smiled at Coward. "We'll run you back to unit command and Intelligence can put a ruler over your story. Doesn't figure to me, but maybe they can make some sense of it. One thing—cut out the sight-seeing. This area's not cleared of Krauts yet and there's no percentage in sticking your necks out."

"Don't worry about that, sir. We'll enjoy the ride."

"Glad to get back, eh?"

"Yes, but it's not only that. We've never seen a jeep before."

It was a wonderful feeling, one they absorbed in a daze. As soon as the preliminary interrogation was over, the intelligence officer led them to the field cookhouse.

"These boys haven't eaten for a year," he announced to the denimed sergeant there. "Fix 'em up, will you?"

"Guess there ain't much left now. Got your irons?"

"Afraid not," replied Harry apologetically.

"Okay, okay. I'll fill a *Kraut* helmet for you. Guess we're out of dessert, though. All I can give you is a couple of cans of pineapple."

"Pineapple!" repeated Coward unbelievingly.

"Sure, what's the beef? There's a war on, ain't there?"

The days were mad, incredible beyond their dreams. Reclining on camp beds in a squad tent when they were not feasting as never before, they surrendered themselves to the overwhelming hospitality of the Americans. Although the unit base was only a mile or two from frontline fighting, no kindness seemed beyond the ingenuity and will of their hosts to shower upon them. Other British ex-prisoners drifted in, until about fifty of them formed a happy band of men drinking in the sweet waters of safety, relaxation, friendship and plenty. Reality seemed very far away with its haggardness and cruelty; yet surely they would awake from this delicious fantasy to find a bayonet-point prodding them from a cold barracks bunk.

Coward hardly noticed the days passing. Then, when the first shock was over, he went to the transport officer.

"You've treated us like blooming kings, but we'd like to know when you can get us back home," he said firmly.

The officer stared. "That's up to you, surely," he said.

"What d'you mean?"

"Well, this show's going forward all the time. Nothing going back except wounded and Kraut prisoners. If you want to go back to the base now, you'll have to make your own way, son."

"How can we do that?"

"I know how I'd do it if I'd got free like you boys have. There are still plenty of German cars around. Why don't you grab what you want and beat it to Brussels? They'll take care of you there."

"That's wonderful. Thanks, thanks a lot!"

"Don't thank me. Give my love to Piccadilly."

"Piccadilly, yes—I can't believe it!"

"But remember: take it easy."

The advice was good, but wasted. There can rarely have been a more hilarious drive than that one. Most of the men quickly found cars, some of them seized on the happy idea of a fire engine, and the whole procession charged its reckless way along the dusty roads, cheering and clanging the bell whenever it passed the convoys moving forward. The whole world was an ecstatic place, boundless with possibilities and empty of any danger. It was a glorious drive, a returning full of incoherent, heart-brimming promise. And a few days later, on April 14th, 1945, an incredulous housewife in the Edmonton district of London looked back at the telegraph boy and made no attempt to check her tears. The laconic message in her hand read:

DARLING ESCAPED FROM GERMANY ARRIVED HERE BY PLANE WILL BE HOME ABOUT FOUR —CHARLIE

EPILOGUE

How could it be true that buses and taxis still thronged the central London streets, that great departmental stores could offer their thousands of variegated luxuries, that one could walk at will into any restaurant or snack bar and enjoy a good meal? There were cigarette and confectionery kiosks, newsstands with today's papers and this week's journal, shops casually displaying such treasures as a pair of scissors, a suit, comfortable shoes, tickets for the theater, books. At the Tube stations there were no *SS* men at the barriers, no passes to be shown; one slipped coppers into a machine and just rode anywhere, filled with the sheer joy of survival. In the miraculous comfort of home, one could bathe every day, listen to family voices, receive a letter written only the day before, eat an apple whenever one liked. Life was very, very good.

Almost before he had regained his breath, the bewildered Cockney who carried in him the indestructibility of London itself was nominated as a Forces candidate for Parliament. He delivered addresses on social security and planning for peace, then withdrew in favor of the Conservative candidate for Edmonton.

But the war was not over for him, or for the particular Germans whom he had sworn to bring to book. Early in 1947 an impressive line of American military staff cars drew up outside his home and disgorged high-ranking legal officers. He was put through a searching examination and Duke Minskoff, shrewd and lightning-witted assistant lawyer to Josiah Dubois, who, in the face of political opposition, had courageously under-

BRAUSEBAD

taken the prosecution of a number of I.G. Farben-industrie officials, asked him if he would be prepared to testify in the war crimes trials. His reply, of course, could never have been in doubt.

The task of Dubois and his team was Herculean. As the Allied armies had commandeered administrative buildings, whole lorryloads of vital documentary evidence had been lost, some simply tossed out of windows to make way for military occupation, some to disappear more mysteriously. But gradually the briefs were assembled, and in October 1946 at Nuremburg the Military Tribunal VI of the United States of America opened "The Farben Case," lasting three years and covering some fifteen thousand pages of testimony alone.

The organization of the tremendous chemical combine, its suspected function of seizing control of industries in "friendly" countries before Hitler's armies marched, made for a case so entangled in legal complexities that the admiration of the entire free world is due to the small band of prosecuting lawyers who struggled on with insufficient data and battled with obstacles not always raised by their racial opponents.

Coward's chief concern was, of course, with the cruelty and extermination carried on at Auschwitz. He read with surprise that not one of the twenty-five I.G. Farben directors ever visited the buna factory, that although they attended building conferences none of them was aware of the existence of gas chambers or that the chambers made full use of Farben's exclusive rights to the "Zyklon B" poison gas. His surprise was even greater on learning that the duties of one defendant included the supply of quilted blankets to all prisoners. Helmut Schneider, of the personnel department at Auschwitz, had, during his three years of office there, never known of the Birkenau camp; he had been astonished to see Auschwitz inmates fight over an apple core he had thrown out of his window; and, yes, he had received one complaint from the International Red Cross—that beer for the English camp should be distributed by the prisoners themselves.

Coward's turn came eleven months after the trials began. Together with Eric Doyle, Douglas Frost and other soldiers who had witnessed barbarities at Auschwitz, he traveled to Nuremberg and found himself seated in the courtroom before a wall map of the plant and camps. Questions from German counsel were interpreted to him through headphones; his answers were spoken into a microphone, while two electric bulbs warned him when to slow down or stop altogether. Newsreel cameras whirred as the vital testimony of his night in Birkenau was read out.

Under cross-examination by defense counsel, he insisted on the existence of the gas chambers, though, not unnaturally, found it difficult to indicate their exact location on the map.

"You said that you went to town every day and that the people in the town, the *SS* men, the concentration camp inmates and the foreign laborers told you that thousands of people were being gassed in Auschwitz. May I ask you this, witness? You went into the town as an AWOL without leave? Isn't that right?"

"I was privileged to visit lots of details, and at Auschwitz I could always travel to Auschwitz for that purpose, whenever it was possible, to buy a few razor blades or boot polish. All I had to do was report to the guard room at *Lager VI* or *Lager VIII,* as the case may be, and a guard would be allotted to me."

A little later Dr. Trabandt for Duerrfeld took over.

"Mr. Coward, you said that at one time you were in camp No. IV, that you stole your way in? Is that right?"

"That is correct, sir."

"That you procured prisoner's clothing through cigarettes, and thus you could get in? Is that right?"

"No, I did not procure the clothing in that way, sir. I made arrangements with one of the inmates to change clothing with him, because I had reason for doing so."

"The prisoners had their heads shaved. By reason of your haircut did you not become conspicuous?"

"It so happened, sir, that whilst I was in Auschwitz

my hair was very, very short for health reasons, and I
should imagine that it would be rather hard to dis-
tinguish between me and the inmates.

"Yes, but you probably looked healthier and had a
better appearance than the inmates. Wouldn't you be
recognized because of that?"

"Well, I don't think so, though I must say I was
perhaps a million per cent more healthy than the inmates. I don't think they were looking to see whether a
man was healthy as he went from work."

"Well, you didn't go to work but you came from
work, and you were probably checked when you came
into the camp. Didn't they notice you by reason of
your different appearance?"

"I don't think so. As I stated, they were not looking
for healthy men to march into camp. Also, I had the
assistance of about three other inmates, who sort of
protected me, inasmuch as I was in about the second
row, you see, and when we were counted the guard
that counted us didn't look at every man to see if he
were English, Irish, Scotch, or Welsh. He would have
had to be a real magician to see that I was English
among those people."

"Very well." Dr. Trabandt continued, trying to confuse him on the number of the bunks in the slaves'
barracks, then retired. Mr. Minskoff rose for a redirect
examination.

"Just one question, Your Honours. With respect to
the British prisoners of war, did you personally ever
make complaints to the management of I.G. Farben?"

"Oh yes, sir. I had contact with Dr. Duerrfeld and
his, shall we say, undermanagers. And Dr. Duerrfeld
very often visited *Lager VI,* once with a group of officers, and on this particular occasion—I don't know
the ranks of these particular officers, but I sort of
imagine they were of very high order, because they
tried their utmost to keep us British prisoners away
from them—I managed to go to the canteen and force
my way in by bluff and complain to all the people that
were there."

"What was the nature of the complaints you made?"

"On this particular occasion, it was regarding bedding, blankets. They had issued us some blankets in *Lager VI* that were made out of—I suppose you say were such that if you happened to move in bed at night you tore it. Even if you would shake the blanket, the blanket would fall to pieces, and the guards or the supervisory officer there, the German officer, they made a particular visit to the rooms to see that everything was all right; he would complain about the wanton, as he called it, destruction of the blankets."

Dr. Seidl, for Duerrfeld, began recross-examination. "Witness, in what camp were you, in No. VIII or No. VI?"

"In both *Lagers*."

"Is it correct to say that both *Lager VIII* and *Lager VI* were guarded by the German *Wehrmacht* and that the entire administration of these camps was in the hands of the German troops?"

"Not the administration, sir, only for discipline. The administration came from Dr. Duerrfeld. The orders that were sent to us were in German and in English and signed by Dr. Duerrfeld. So, therefore, Dr. Duerrfeld was the man that we naturally took to be the boss of the show."

On the same day Norbert Wollheim, a former inmate, gave evidence of his own experiences, never having seen his wife and child again since they were separated at Auschwitz, and described the intense hardship of work imposed by Duerrfeld. But when the latter's turn came, it was quite a different story.

Walter Duerrfeld, chief of construction and installation at Auschwitz and a director of the plant, had never heard anything about systematic extermination; indeed, when the war ended, he had been working on a scheme by which inmates could draw up their own menu each day.

"Didn't you ever suspect," asked his counsel, "that inmates, unfit for work, might be pushed off from Camp IV to Auschwitz or Birkenau or some other camp in order to be liquidated?"

"Dr. Seidl," protested Duerrfeld, "this horrible

thought never occurred to us." Questioned about the inmates' physical appearance, he explained that if "very many of them had care written on their faces, then I can only say that my heart bled. . . . If one saw them at their place of work, Dr. Seidl, if one looked at one individual working and if one saw that he was desperate and loaded down with cares, then I could not pass by this man without showing him that one had compassion with his fate." Ten square miles of camps, he pointed out, was a very large area and not even rumors of any gassings had ever reached his ears; indeed, until this trial he had not been clear about the existence of a place called Birkenau. "I did nobody any harm, nor did I order anybody to be harmed. I deprived nobody of liberty," he said in his final statement. "Nobody lost life or health pursuant to directives issued by the plant, and wherever within the jurisdiction of the plant I saw or heard of an injustice I destroyed it in its very roots. . . . I feel only too clearly and it is the case to-day, more than at any other time, that the world will not achieve its aim of peace unless men learn to forgive one another." He was found not guilty.

The noise and clamor of "The Farben Case" was still echoing, the successes and crushing disappointments still being hotly debated, when in January of 1953 a letter reached Coward from Henry Ormond, a lawyer in Frankfurt.

> *I am conducting a law unit for Mr. Norbert Wollheim, formerly Lübeck, now New York, U.S.A., versus I.G. Farbenindustrie for compensation. The case concerns Mr. Wollheim's claim for compensation for the forced labor he had to perform as an Auschwitz concentration inmate in the I.G. Farben buna plant at Buna-Monowitz from March 1943 till January 1945. This is a test case which will enable a great number of other concentration camp inmates who escaped the Auschwitz hell to raise similar claims.*
>
> *The case is pending before the Frankfurt Court. A number of witnesses from Germany and from abroad*

*have been heard in the course of the last few months.
The Court has now expressed the wish to hear one or
two former British P.O.W.s as especially impartial
and objective witnesses. I have seen your affidavits
and your statements in the Nuremberg I.G. Farben
Trial and I therefore would very much like to invite
you to appear in February here.*

At last here was the chance to do something posi-
tive to help. Coward immediately cabled his willingness
to attend, and in mid-February he and Robert Ferris,
another British witness who had helped with the sabotage at Auschwitz, flew to Frankfurt, finding at the air-
port a battery of photographers, for this was one of
the most important civil actions ever heard. The worm
had turned: a slave with less acknowledged rights than
his master would give to a dog, a man torn from his
family for ever and subjected to more humiliation and
savagery than it seems possible that a human being
could bear, was taking due process of law to gain retribution.

As Coward's evidence was given, his picture was
flashed to newspapers all over the world. The interpreter almost fainted when he described how he had
been obliged to gather his information at Auschwitz.
His statement of the conditions of living suffered by
inmates, as witnessed by his own night of hell, and his
stubborn refusal to be shaken when under the fire of
cross-examination, proved to be the turning point of
the case. It was one of the happiest days of his life
when, in June that year, a telegram arrived at his home
from the brilliant, untiring lawyer who had made it all
possible.

VICTORY TEN THOUSAND MARKS GO TO NOR-
BERT WOLLHEIM JUDGMENT MENTIONS YOU
AND FERRIS FREQUENTLY YOUR EVIDENCE IM-
PRESSED THEM—HENRY ORMOND —

They had indeed been mentioned frequently. Re-
marking on Coward's bravery, the judgment termed

him "a man who dared to do something for the Jewish prisoners, thereby showing great moral courage. He did this for the mere reason that *he and the prisoners were fellow human beings,* although, he might, with a greater degree of justification than the witnesses for the defendants, have adopted the attitude that he was not concerned with the fate of the plaintiff, and might have claimed that he "was not competent," that it "was not his province," and so forth—terms which recur with startling frequency in the evidence of the witnesses for the defendants examined early in the proceedings. . . .

"The Chamber is inclined to explain the attitude adopted by the defendants at that time by the fact that their exponents, especially in 1943, in actual fact did not look upon the plaintiff and the Jewish prisoners as people entitled to the rights of human beings, or else did not or could not muster the requisite moral courage they were obliged to show as employers, or at least as those actually wielding all power. The fact that a British prisoner of war had to show the German defendants what moral courage involved is a matter of regret to the Chamber as a German Court."

Letters began to shower on Coward from societies for the exiled and oppressed. Typical of several, one of them from the Association of Jewish Refugees in Great Britain, read:

We are writing to you as the representative organization of the Jewish Nazi victims from Germany and Austria who were admitted to this country before the outbreak of the war and who were thus spared the unspeakable plight of their nearest ones they had to leave behind. After having received the full wording of the Frankfurt I.G. Farben judgment we feel urged to point out to you how deeply we were impressed by the humane spirit and courageous attitude displayed by you and Mr. Ferris during your imprisonment in the Monowitz camp. We know only too well from the reports which have transpired since the end of the war what our people had to endure in the camps. Apart

*from physical sufferings the worst for them was cer-
tainly the fact that they were helplessly exposed to the
cruelty of their persecutors. It will therefore have
helped them to retain their belief in humanity if their
burden was eased by men like you and Mr. Ferris.—
Yours very truly.* (signed) *H. Reichmann, Chairman;*
(signed) *W. Rosenstock, General Secretary.*

It was much later, in April of 1954, and Coward
was enjoying a quiet drink in his favorite Edmonton
pub, the Rose and Crown, when the landlord leaned
toward him with a newspaper in his hand.

"Seen the *Manchester Guardian,* Charlie?" he asked.
"Got a big write-up—'Slave-labor claims against firms.'
That was your do, wasn't it—all that Farben business?"

"That's right. Must be Farben's appeal starting
soon."

"Gawd, I've been reading it. Fair makes your hair
stand on end. Appears they got infected lice from the
prisoners and supplied 'em to some scientific institute
in Poland. Court couldn't prove genocide, though."

"No," said Coward. "There were a lot of things the
court couldn't prove, even though everybody knew
about the medical experiments that went on all the
time. You wouldn't believe them, if I told you. But
what does it say about the appeal?"

"Just a sec—there's yards of it. 'Consternation has
been caused throughout West German industry by the
increasing danger of claims running into thousands of
millions of marks being made against all firms who
employed slave labor during the war and who failed
either to pay or treat their workers properly. A number
of German firms, led by the successors of the great
I.G. Farben chemical combine, have enlisted a team
of the best lawyers in Europe to defend their interests.
This team is believed to include German lawyers who
took part in the defense of the war criminals in Span-
dau and the best American legal counsel available in
Europe.' "

"Too true. Even Farben can't stand claims like that
if Wollheim wins."

"Yes, but it's not only Farben. It says this Wollheim case has opened up claims against the other big German industrial concerns—Krupps and suchlike. Although Farben are the biggest. Listen: 'I.G. Farben is playing a leading part in this affair, because claims for damages have already been brought against the firm, and one of them has been upheld by a Frankfurt court. Since this happened in June about two thousand suits against I.G. Farben alone have filed.' Two thousand! And it says that a lot more are expected, because about twenty thousand Jews managed to survive the concentration and forced labor camps. Just think of it, Charlie." The publican put down the paper and wiped his forehead. "Twenty thousand of them who may be able to bring a case."

Into Coward's mind there came a picture of the heaped-up bodies of some of the millions of inmates who had not survived.

"That's pretty good, Perce," he said quietly, pushing his empty glass across the bar counter. "Here, you'd better have one with me."

BANTAM WAR BOOKS

Now there is a great new series of carefully selected books that together cover the full dramatic sweep of World War II heroism—viewed from all sides and representing all branches of armed service, whether on land, sea or in the air. All of the books are true stories of brave men and women. Most volumes are eyewitness accounts by those who fought in the conflict. Many of the books are already famous bestsellers.

Each book in this series contains a powerful fold-out full-color painting typifying the subject of the books; many have been specially commissioned. There are also specially commissioned identification illustrations of aircraft, weapons, vehicles, and other equipment, which accompany the text for greater understanding, plus specially commissioned maps and charts to explain unusual terrain, fighter plane tactics, and step-by-step progress of battles. Also included are carefully compiled indexes and bibliographies as an aid to further reading.